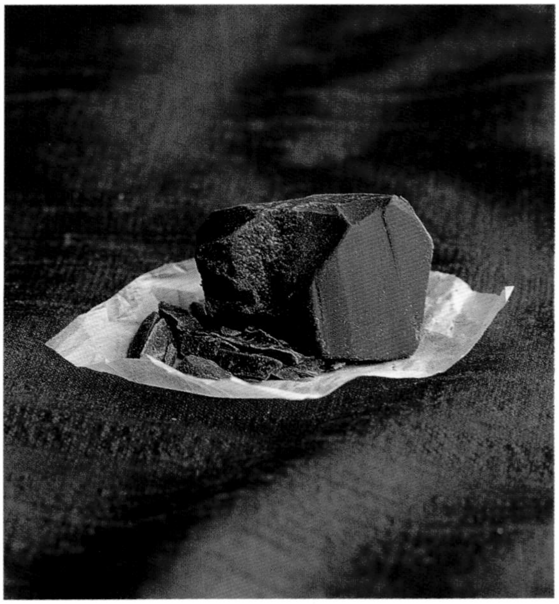

WILLIAMS-SONOMA

DESSERT

RECIPES AND TEXT
ABIGAIL JOHNSON DODGE

GENERAL EDITOR
CHUCK WILLIAMS

PHOTOGRAPHS
MAREN CARUSO

SIMON & SCHUSTER • SOURCE

NEW YORK • LONDON • TORONTO • SYDNEY • SINGAPORE

CONTENTS

HOLIDAY DESSERTS

SPECIAL OCCASIONS

CHOCOLATE DECADENCE

INTRODUCTION

A homemade dessert is always appreciated. It's the extra step a cook can take that turns an ordinary meal into something special. In this cookbook, we've put together a range of recipes for every occasion, taste, and skill level. There's a chapter of simple desserts that come together in minutes as well as the classic pies, cakes, and mousses that should be included in every cook's repertoire. Delicious fruit desserts celebrate the spectacular offerings of summer, while a selection of decadent chocolate desserts may just prove irresistible to even the busiest cook.

Best of all, these kitchen-tested recipes guarantee success every time, so you won't be disappointed. Each recipe is accompanied by a side note that highlights a particular ingredient or cooking technique, broadening your knowledge in the kitchen, while a chapter of baking basics clearly lays out everything you need to know to get started. It is my wish that Williams-Sonoma's *Dessert* will bring a little sweetness to your table.

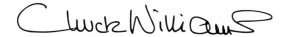

THE CLASSICS

Here's a collection of old favorites that are also irresistible, which means they will never go out of fashion in anyone's kitchen. These are indispensable recipes, the ones you will turn to again and again, from a seasonal fruit tart and luscious chocolate cake to a high-rising soufflé and rich cheesecake. All make lovely presentations, and all are absolutely delicious.

FLOURLESS CHOCOLATE TORTE

CHOCOLATE GLAZE

To make the glaze, combine ½ cup butter (4 oz/125 g), cut into 4 pieces, and 8 oz (250 g) chopped bittersweet chocolate in the top of a double boiler (page 106). Set over barely simmering water and melt, then whisk until blended. Remove from the heat and whisk in 2 tablespoons light corn syrup until smooth and glossy. Set the cold cake on a wire rack over a large plate or baking sheet. Slowly pour the warm glaze over the center of the cake. The glaze should cover the surface evenly, spilling over the edges and running down the sides, the excess falling onto the plate below.

Preheat the oven to 300°F (150°C). Grease the bottom of an 8-inch (20-cm) round cake pan and line it with parchment (baking) paper. Grease the paper and the sides of the pan, then dust with cocoa powder.

In the top of a double boiler (page 106), combine the chocolate and the ¾ cup butter. Set over barely simmering water and melt, then whisk until well blended. Set aside to cool slightly.

In a large bowl, with a mixer set on medium-high speed, beat together the egg yolks, ¼ cup sugar, dark rum (if using), vanilla, and salt until pale and very thick. Gradually pour in the chocolate mixture and continue beating until well blended.

In deep, clean bowl, using a mixer on medium-high speed, beat the egg whites until foamy. Gradually add the remaining sugar and continue to beat until medium-firm peaks form. Scoop half of the egg whites onto the chocolate mixture and fold them in gently. Fold in the remaining whites just until no streaks remain.

Pour the batter into the prepared pan and spread it out evenly. Bake the torte until it puffs slightly and a toothpick inserted into the center comes out very moist but not liquid, about 35 minutes. Do not overcook. Let cool on a rack for 30 minutes.

Run a small knife around the inside of the pan to loosen the cake, then invert onto a flat plate. Lift off the pan and carefully peel off the parchment paper. Let cool completely. Cover and refrigerate until very cold, at least 4 hours or up to overnight.

Glaze the cake with the chocolate glaze *(left),* then refrigerate again until firm, at least 2 hours. Transfer to a flat serving plate. Using a thin-bladed knife, cut the cake into small slices, dipping the knife into hot water and wiping it dry before each cut.

MAKES ONE 8-INCH (20-CM) CAKE. OR 10 SERVINGS

Unsweetened cocoa powder for dusting

10 oz (315 g) bittersweet chocolate, finely chopped

¾ cup (6 oz/185 g) unsalted butter, cut into 6 pieces, plus extra for greasing

5 large egg yolks

¼ cup (1¾ oz/50 g) plus 2 tablespoons sugar

1 tablespoon dark rum or brewed espresso (optional)

1 teaspoon vanilla extract (essence)

Pinch of salt

3 large egg whites, at room temperature

Chocolate Glaze *(far left)*

TARTE TATIN

Basic Pastry Dough (page 113), chilled

¼ cup (2 oz/60 g) unsalted butter, cut into 4 pieces

¾ cup (5¼ oz/160 g) sugar

5 Golden Delicious or other baking or all-purpose apples *(far right),* about 2 lb (1 kg) total weight, peeled, quartered lengthwise, and cored

Vanilla ice cream for serving (optional)

Lightly dust a work surface and a rolling pin with flour. Roll out the chilled dough into a 12-inch (30-cm) round, a scant ¼ inch (6 mm) thick. Lift and turn the dough several times as you roll to prevent sticking, and dust the surface and the rolling pin with additional flour as needed. Use a dough scraper or icing spatula to loosen the pastry if it sticks. Trim the dough into an 11-inch (28-cm) round. Slide a rimless baking sheet under the dough, cover with plastic, and refrigerate until needed.

Preheat the oven to 375°F (190°C) and select a 10-inch (25-cm), straight-sided, ovenproof frying pan, preferably cast iron. Place it over medium heat and heat the butter. When it melts, sprinkle the sugar evenly over the butter and continue cooking until the sugar melts and turns amber-colored, 3–4 minutes. Shake and swirl the frying pan frequently to redistribute the sugar for even melting and caramelization.

Arrange the apples, core side up, in the caramel in a snug, even layer. Raise the heat to medium-high and cook until the apples are just tender, about 15 minutes. The caramel will bubble up around the apples. Remove the pan from the heat.

Uncover the pastry round. When the bubbling has subsided, slide both hands under the pastry round and carefully place it on top of the apples, tucking in the edges and being careful not to burn your fingers. Bake until the crust is golden brown, about 30 minutes.

Let cool on a rack for 5 minutes. Place a large flat serving plate upside down on top of the pan and invert the pan and plate together. Lift off the pan. Slice and serve warm with vanilla ice cream, if desired.

MAKES ONE 10-INCH (25-CM) TART, OR 8 SERVINGS

APPLES FOR BAKING
Which apple variety to select for a recipe depends on how the fruit will be used. Apples fall into three broad groups. Sauce apples, such as the Cortland and McIntosh, collapse readily, turning into applesauce after little more than a brief simmer. Baking apples, such as Golden Delicious *(above),* Rome Beauty, and Pink Lady, hold their shape beautifully for up to an hour in the oven. Any baking apple may be used in this recipe. All-purpose apples, like the Granny Smith, have a texture when cooked that falls between tender and firm and might also be used for this recipe.

GRAND MARNIER SOUFFLÉ

FOR THE PASTRY CREAM:

1 cup (8 fl oz/250 ml) whole milk

6 large eggs, separated, at room temperature

2/3 cup (4 2/3 oz/145 g) sugar

3 tablespoons all-purpose (plain) flour

2 teaspoons finely grated orange zest

Pinch of salt

1/4 cup (2 fl oz/60 ml) Grand Marnier or other orange liqueur

1 teaspoon vanilla extract (essence)

Unsalted butter for greasing

Sugar for dusting

Crème Anglaise (page 113) for serving

To make the pastry cream, in a saucepan over medium heat, warm the milk until small bubbles appear along the edge of the pan. Remove from the heat. In a bowl, whisk together the egg yolks, 1/3 cup (2 1/3 oz/70 g) of the sugar, the flour, the zest, and the salt until pale and well blended. Slowly add the hot milk while whisking. Pour the mixture back into the saucepan and place over medium-low heat. Cook, whisking constantly, until the mixture comes to a boil. Continue to cook, whisking constantly, for 1 minute. Remove from the heat and whisk in the liqueur and vanilla. Pour the pastry cream into a large bowl and gently press a piece of plastic wrap directly onto the surface to prevent a skin from forming. Let cool to room temperature or refrigerate until ready to bake.

Preheat the oven to 375°F (190°C). Lightly grease a 6-cup (48–fl oz/ 1.5-l) soufflé dish and dust with sugar.

Remove the plastic wrap from the pastry cream and whisk until smooth. In a deep, spotlessly clean bowl, using a mixer set on medium-high speed, beat the egg whites until they are foamy and soft peaks form when the beaters are lifted. Gradually add the remaining 1/3 cup sugar while beating, and continue to beat until stiff peaks form.

Scoop about one-fourth of the egg whites onto the pastry cream and, using a rubber spatula, fold in gently to lighten the mixture. Then fold in the remaining whites just until no white streaks remain. Scoop into the prepared dish. Run a thumb around the inside rim of the dish to keep the batter from sticking and help the soufflé rise.

Bake until the soufflé is puffed and the top is browned, but the soufflé still jiggles slightly when the dish is gently shaken, about 30 minutes. Serve immediately with the crème anglaise.

MAKES 6–8 SERVINGS

SOUFFLÉ SAVVY

A soufflé, whose name derives from the French verb "to blow," is an airy concoction leavened by beaten egg whites and oven heat. Soufflés should be served directly from the oven, before they have any chance to deflate. The soufflé dish, a ceramic dish with tall, straight sides, is usually greased and then dusted with sugar (or, for savory soufflés, bread crumbs) to help the batter "climb" the sides of the dish. For some high-rising soufflés, a collar is fashioned out of parchment (baking) paper to give more support. For more details, see pages 67 and 85.

RASPBERRY TART

Basic Pastry Dough, chilled and rolled into a 13-inch (33-cm) round, ⅛ inch (3 mm) thick (page 113)

FOR THE PASTRY CREAM:

1 cup (8 fl oz/250 ml) whole milk

2 large eggs, at room temperature

¼ cup (1¾ oz/50 g) sugar

4 teaspoons cornstarch (cornflour)

Pinch of salt

1 teaspoon vanilla extract (essence)

¼ cup (2 fl oz/60 ml) heavy (double) cream

3–4 cups (¾–1 lb/375–500 g) raspberries

Fruit Glaze *(far right)*

Carefully transfer the rolled-out pastry dough round to a 9½-inch (24-cm) tart pan with a removable bottom, gently fitting the dough into the pan without stretching. Trim the edges, leaving a ½-inch (12-mm) overhang. Fold the overhang back over itself and press it into the sides of the pan, creating a double thickness to reinforce the sides of the tart. Freeze until the shell is firm, 30 minutes.

Preheat the oven to 425°F (220°C). Line the frozen shell with foil and fill with pie weights or dried beans. Bake for 15 minutes. Remove the weights and foil and continue to bake until the shell is pale gold, 4–5 minutes longer. Let cool completely on a rack.

To make the pastry cream, in a saucepan over medium heat, warm the milk until small bubbles appear along the edge of the pan. Remove from the heat. In a bowl, whisk together the eggs, sugar, cornstarch, and salt. Slowly add the hot milk while whisking. Pour the mixture back into the pan and place over medium-low heat. Cook, whisking constantly, until the mixture comes to a boil and thickens. Continue to cook, whisking constantly, for 20 seconds. Pour into a clean bowl and gently press a piece of plastic wrap directly onto the surface to prevent a skin from forming. Refrigerate until cold, for at least 2 hours or up to 24 hours.

Whisk the vanilla into the chilled pastry cream until blended and smooth. In another bowl, using a mixer on medium-high speed, whip the cream until firm peaks form. Fold the whipped cream into the pastry cream until just blended.

To assemble the tart, spoon the pastry cream into the cooled tart shell and spread evenly. Arrange the raspberries randomly on top of the cream. Brush the berries with the fruit glaze. Cut the tart into slender wedges and serve.

MAKES ONE 9½-INCH (24-CM) TART, OR 10–12 SERVINGS

FRUIT GLAZE
A simple glaze made from jelly diluted with water gives fresh fruit tart fillings a lovely sheen and a finished look. In a small saucepan, combine ¼ cup (2½ oz/75 g) apple jelly or seedless raspberry jelly with 2 tablespoons water. Set the pan over low heat and cook, stirring the mixture constantly, until melted and smooth. Remove from the heat and let cool slightly. Using a small pastry brush or feather brush, dab the glaze onto the fruit.

VANILLA CHEESECAKE

FORMING THE CRUST
A crumb crust is classic for cheesecake. After creating the crumb mixture, pour it into the prepared pan. Spread the crumbs around the bottom of the pan, leaving any crumbs that stick to the sides of the pan where they are. Using a straight-sided, flat-bottomed coffee mug, press against the crumbs from the center outward to form an even layer on the bottom and up the sides of the pan. You can also use your hand, wrapping it in a plastic bag to keep crumbs from sticking to your fingers.

To make the crust, preheat the oven to 400°F (200°C). Lightly grease a 9-inch (23-cm) springform pan. In a bowl, combine the graham cracker crumbs, sugar, cinnamon, and melted butter. Stir until the mixture is well blended and the crumbs are evenly moist. Pour into the springform pan and press evenly onto the bottom and about 1½ inches (4 cm) up the sides of the pan *(left)*. Bake until lightly golden and set, about 10 minutes. Let cool on a rack. Reduce the oven temperature to 300°F (150°C).

To make the filling, in a large bowl, combine the cream cheese, flour, and salt. Using a mixer set on medium-high speed, beat until very smooth and fluffy, stopping and scraping down the sides frequently. Add the sugar, sour cream, and vanilla. Beat until well blended, again scraping down the sides frequently. Add the eggs one at a time, beating well after each addition. Pour into the crust.

Bake the cheesecake until the filling is set but the center still jiggles slightly when the pan is gently shaken and the edges are slightly puffed, 60–70 minutes. The filling will firm as it cools. Let cool on a rack to room temperature. Cover and refrigerate until well chilled (overnight is best).

To serve, unclasp and remove the pan sides, then run a long, thin icing spatula between the pan bottom and the crust. Carefully slide the cake onto a flat serving plate. Using a thin-bladed knife, cut the cake into slices, dipping the knife into hot water and wiping it dry before each cut.

MAKES ONE 9-INCH (23-CM) CHEESECAKE, OR 16 SERVINGS

FOR THE CRUST:

1½ cups (4½ oz/140 g) graham cracker crumbs

3 tablespoons sugar

½ teaspoon ground cinnamon

¼ cup (2 oz/60 g) unsalted butter, melted, plus extra for greasing

FOR THE FILLING:

4 packages (8 oz/250 g each) cream cheese, at room temperature

2 tablespoons all-purpose (plain) flour

¼ teaspoon salt

1¼ cups (8¾ oz/270 g) sugar

½ cup (4 oz/125 g) sour cream

1 tablespoon vanilla extract (essence)

3 large eggs, at room temperature

CRÈME BRÛLÉE

3 cups (24 fl oz/750 ml)
heavy (double) cream

½ vanilla bean, split
lengthwise *(far right)*

8 large egg yolks, at room
temperature

½ cup (3½ oz/105 g) plus
⅓ cup (2⅓ oz/70 g) sugar

Preheat the oven to 300°F (150°C). Have ready six ¾-cup (6–fl oz/ 180-ml) ramekins and a shallow roasting pan.

In a saucepan over medium heat, combine the cream and vanilla bean. Bring to a gentle boil, remove from the heat, cover, and set aside for 15–30 minutes to blend the flavors. Remove the vanilla bean from the cream and, using the tip of a knife, scrape the seeds into the cream. Discard the bean or save for another use *(right)*.

Return the cream to medium heat and bring almost to a boil. Remove from the heat. In a bowl, whisk together the egg yolks and the ⅓ cup sugar just until blended. Slowly whisk in the hot cream. Return the mixture to the saucepan over medium-low heat. Cook, stirring constantly, until the custard is thick enough to coat the back of a spoon, about 3 minutes. Do not let it boil. Pour the custard through a strainer into the ramekins, dividing it evenly among them.

Arrange the ramekins in the roasting pan. Pour very hot tap water into the pan to come halfway up the sides of the ramekins. Cover the pan with aluminum foil. Bake until the custards are set but the centers still jiggle slightly when the ramekins are gently shaken, about 40 minutes. Remove from the oven but leave in the water bath until cool enough to handle, then lift out the ramekins. Cover and refrigerate until well chilled, up to overnight.

Just before serving, preheat the broiler (grill). Sift the remaining ½ cup sugar over the tops of the chilled custards to form a thin, even layer and place the ramekins on a baking sheet. Slip the baking sheet under the broiler 2–3 inches (5–7.5 cm) from the heat source and broil (grill) until the sugar melts and caramelizes, 1–2 minutes. Turn the ramekins as needed to cook the sugar evenly. Alternatively, use a small kitchen blowtorch to caramelize the sugar. Serve immediately.

MAKES 6 SERVINGS

VANILLA BEANS

A vanilla bean is the cured pod of a type of climbing orchid. For the best flavor, choose plump, dark pods showing no signs of shriveling. Most recipes call for a whole or half bean split lengthwise. Splitting the pod allows the tiny seeds to escape and their flavor to permeate a dish. If infusing liquids with vanilla, steep the split bean in the liquid, then remove the pod and scrape the seeds into the liquid. The pod can be used again, although its flavor will be less intense. Once dry, a leftover bean may be buried in a jar of sugar to give the sugar a subtle vanilla flavor.

ANGEL FOOD CAKE WITH STRAWBERRY TOPPING

Preheat the oven to 350°F (180°C). Have ready an ungreased 10-inch (25-cm) angel food cake pan lined with parchment paper.

Sift together the flour, 1 cup (7 oz/220 g) of the superfine sugar, and the salt 3 times and set aside. In a large, spotlessly clean bowl, using a mixer set on medium-low speed, beat the egg whites until foamy. Add the cream of tartar, increase the speed to medium-high, and beat until the whites are soft and foamy. Gradually add the remaining superfine sugar and continue to beat just until medium-firm peaks form when the beaters are lifted. Do not overbeat. Stir in the lemon juice, vanilla, and zest, if using.

Transfer the egg mixture to a very large bowl. Sift a fourth of the flour mixture over it, and using a large rubber spatula, gently fold it into the egg whites using deep strokes. Add the remaining flour mixture in 3 equal batches, sifting and folding each time. Scoop the batter into the pan and gently smooth the top. Bake until the cake is golden and springs back when touched, about 40 minutes. Remove from the oven and invert the pan onto its feet or the neck of a wine bottle. Let cool completely.

Meanwhile, to make the topping, combine the berries, granulated sugar, and lemon juice in a saucepan over high heat. Bring to a boil, stirring often. Boil until the liquid is clear and somewhat thick, 2 minutes. Pour into a clean bowl and refrigerate until chilled.

To remove the cake from the pan, gently run a long, thin-bladed knife around the outer sides of the pan, pressing it firmly against the pan to prevent tearing the cake. Then run the knife or a skewer around the inside of the tube. Invert the pan and let the cake slide out. Remove the paper lining. Using a serrated knife, cut into slices. Serve each slice with a spoonful of strawberry topping.

MAKES ABOUT 10 SERVINGS

SEPARATING EGGS

Eggs are easier to separate when they are cold. Carefully crack each egg and, holding it over a bowl, pass the yolk back and forth between the shell halves and let the whites fall into the bowl. Drop the yolk into a separate bowl, and transfer the whites to a third bowl. Separate each additional egg over an empty bowl, for if any speck of yolk gets into the whites, the whites will not whip up properly. If a yolk breaks, start fresh with another egg. Let the separated egg whites come to room temperature before using them in the batter.

1 cup (4 oz/125 g) cake (soft-wheat) flour

1¼ cups (8¾ oz/270 g) superfine (caster) sugar

¼ teaspoon salt

1¼ cups (10 fl oz/310 ml) egg whites (about 10 large eggs), at room temperature

1½ teaspoons cream of tartar

2 teaspoons fresh lemon juice

1 teaspoon vanilla extract (essence)

1 teaspoon finely grated lemon zest (optional)

FOR THE TOPPING:

4 cups (1 lb/500 g) strawberries, hulled and thickly sliced

¼ cup (1¾ oz/50 g) granulated sugar

2 tablespoons fresh lemon juice

SIMPLE DESSERTS

It makes sense to have a few wonderful yet simple desserts in your repertoire—dishes that are quick and uncomplicated or that can be whipped up from just a handful of ingredients. Although these recipes are straightforward and undemanding, they are still full of flavor and good enough for company. A little whipped cream and some fresh fruit are all they need to be at their Sunday best.

BREAD PUDDING

Lightly grease an 8-inch (20-cm) square baking dish. Spread the bread cubes in it.

In a bowl, whisk together the eggs, brown sugar, vanilla, cinnamon, nutmeg, and salt until well blended. Pour in the milk and whisk until combined. Pour the mixture over the bread cubes. Let sit, pressing down on the bread occasionally, until the bread is evenly soaked, about 20 minutes.

Meanwhile, preheat the oven to 350°F (180°C). Have ready a large, shallow roasting pan.

Scatter the cranberries evenly over the surface of the soaked bread and press to submerge the fruit. Set the baking dish in the roasting pan. Add very hot tap water to the roasting pan to come halfway up the sides of the baking dish.

Bake the pudding until a knife inserted near the center comes out almost clean, 45–55 minutes. Serve warm or at room temperature, with a generous dusting of confectioners' sugar over the top of each slice.

MAKES 8 SERVINGS

BREAD FOR PUDDING

A simple bread pudding is the perfect use for a day-old baguette or coarse country loaf. These breads have a similar texture and both have a rather bland flavor when stale—the perfect foil for a flavorful custard. Cut the bread into ¾-inch (2-cm) slices, then cut again into ¾-inch (2-cm) cubes. These bite-sized pieces are perfect for soaking up all the custard, yet still hold together well enough to give the dessert some texture.

Unsalted butter for greasing

12 slices day-old baguette, cut into ¾-inch (2-cm) cubes (about 6 cups/12 oz/375 g)

4 large eggs, at room temperature

½ cup (4 oz/125 g) firmly packed light brown sugar

¾ teaspoon vanilla extract (essence)

½ teaspoon ground cinnamon

Pinch of freshly grated nutmeg

Pinch of salt

4 cups (32 fl oz/1 l) whole milk

¼ cup (1½ oz/45 g) dried cranberries or raisins

Confectioners' (icing) sugar for garnish

BERRY FOOL

7 small strawberries, plus 2 small strawberries, halved (optional)

⅓ cup (2⅓ oz/70 g) sugar, plus more to taste

¾ cup (3 oz/90 g) raspberries or blueberries, or a mixture

1 teaspoon fresh lemon juice

Pinch of salt

¾ cup (6 fl oz/180 ml) heavy (double) cream, well chilled

8 small fresh mint leaves for garnish (optional)

Stem and hull the 7 strawberries, then quarter them lengthwise (you should have about ¾ cup/3 oz/90 g). In a small bowl, toss together the quartered strawberries and the ⅓ cup sugar. Then, using a fork, smash the berries until they are jamlike and mostly puréed. Add the raspberries or blueberries and crush lightly with the fork. Stir in the lemon juice and salt. Taste and add 1–2 more tablespoons sugar, if desired. Place in the freezer and chill, stirring frequently, until very cold, about 15 minutes.

In a chilled bowl, using a mixer on medium to medium-high speed, whip the cream until firm peaks form when the beaters are lifted. Scoop the chilled fruit onto the cream and, using a rubber spatula, fold the fruit into the cream until just incorporated.

Serve immediately or cover and refrigerate overnight. Spoon into dessert bowls or glasses. Garnish with the small strawberries and mint leaves, if desired.

MAKES 4 SERVINGS

SERVING FOOL

Berry fool is an old-fashioned English treat whose name derives from the French word *fouler*, to crush. This versatile dessert can be spooned into dessert bowls or wineglasses and served immediately. It also makes a delicious accompaniment to a thin slice of pound cake or angel food cake. Or, for a more showy, but equally easy, presentation, layer the fool in tall wineglasses, alternating it with layers of mixed berries such as sliced strawberries and whole raspberries and blueberries *(above)*.

BROWNIES

Preheat the oven to 350°F (180°C). Lightly grease an 8-inch (20-cm) square baking dish, preferably glass.

In a saucepan over low heat, combine the butter and chopped unsweetened chocolate. Heat, stirring often, until melted, about 4 minutes. Remove from the heat and stir in the sugar and salt. Add the eggs and vanilla and stir until well blended. Sprinkle the sifted flour over the mixture and stir until just blended. Stir in the chips, if using.

Pour the batter into the prepared dish and spread evenly. Bake the brownies until a toothpick inserted into the center comes out almost completely clean, about 30 minutes, or longer if using a metal pan. Do not overbake. Transfer to a wire rack to cool completely before cutting into 2½-inch (6-cm) squares.

MAKES 9 LARGE BROWNIES

½ cup (4 oz/125 g) unsalted butter, cut into 4 pieces, plus extra for greasing

3 oz (90 g) unsweetened chocolate, finely chopped

1 cup (7 oz/220 g) sugar

Pinch of salt

2 large eggs, at room temperature

1 teaspoon vanilla extract (essence)

¾ cup (3 oz/90 g) cake (soft-wheat) flour, sifted

¾ cup (4½ oz/140 g) bittersweet chocolate chips, semisweet (plain) chocolate chips, peanut butter chips, or white chocolate chips (optional)

CHOCOLATE TYPES
Chocolate is categorized by how much chocolate liquor it contains. Unsweetened, or bitter, chocolate is 100 percent chocolate liquor with no sugar added. Bittersweet and semisweet (plain) chocolates have cocoa butter and sugar added to the liquor but still contain at least 35 percent and 15 percent liquor, respectively. In most cases these 2 chocolates are interchangeable in recipes. Milk chocolate, which contains at least 10 percent chocolate liquor and 12 percent milk solids, behaves differently in recipes and should not be used in place of other types of chocolate unless specified.

POUND CAKE

1½ cups (6¾ oz/205 g) all-purpose (plain) flour, plus extra for dusting

¼ teaspoon baking soda (bicarbonate of soda)

¼ teaspoon salt

¾ cup (6 oz/185 g) unsalted butter, at room temperature, plus extra for greasing

1 cup (7 oz/220 g) sugar

1½ teaspoons vanilla extract (essence)

¼ teaspoon almond extract (essence) (optional)

2 large eggs, at room temperature

½ cup (4 oz/125 g) sour cream, at room temperature

Preheat the oven to 325°F (165°C). Lightly grease a 8½-by-4½-inch (21.5-by-11.5-cm) loaf pan, preferably glass, and dust with flour.

In a bowl, whisk together the flour, baking soda, and salt until blended. In another bowl, using a mixer on medium to medium-high speed, beat together the butter, sugar, vanilla, and almond extract (if using) until light and fluffy. Add the eggs one at a time, beating well after each addition, until just blended. Sprinkle half of the flour mixture over the egg mixture and stir until both are just incorporated. Stir in the sour cream, then sprinkle with the remaining flour mixture and stir until evenly distributed.

Pour the batter into the prepared pan and tap gently on the counter to even out and settle the ingredients. Bake until a toothpick inserted into the center comes out clean, about 70 minutes, or longer if using a metal pan. Let cool on a rack for 15 minutes.

Run a thin knife around the inside of the pan, invert the cake onto a wire rack, and lift off the pan. Place the cake on one of its sides and continue cooling. Serve warm or at room temperature.

MAKES 8–10 SERVINGS

POUND CAKE VARIATIONS

A slice of pound cake is buttery, rich, and delicious all by itself, but it takes well to additions, too. Vary this cake's flavor by omitting the almond extract and stirring in 1 teaspoon finely grated lemon zest, 2 tablespoons fresh lemon juice, and 1 tablespoon poppy seeds, or 2 tablespoons minced crystallized ginger. If you like almond, add the optional almond extract and sprinkle sliced (flaked) almonds on top before baking. You can also layer pound cake slices with Chocolate Mousse (page 94) or Berry Fool (page 29), or top the slices with fresh fruit.

STRAWBERRY SHORTCAKES

SHORTCAKE DOUGH

When properly mixed, shortcake dough should be rough, even shaggy. You might be tempted to mix it more, but resist, or you won't end up with a flaky biscuit. Work the dough on a lightly floured work surface, gently pressing and patting it into a thick rectangle. Incorporating too much flour will make the dough tough. Cutting the dough into squares is preferable to rounds. Rounds leave scraps, which must be patted back together to form more cakes. The result is overworked dough and a few tough shortcakes. Squares will all turn out equally tender and delicious.

To make the shortcakes, preheat the oven to 400°F (200°C). Have ready an ungreased baking sheet.

In a bowl, whisk together the flour, sugar, baking powder, zest, and salt until well blended. Using a pastry blender, cut in the butter until the pieces are no larger than peas. Add the buttermilk and vanilla and gently toss with a fork or rubber spatula until the flour is just moistened and the ingredients are blended.

Turn the shaggy dough out onto a lightly floured work surface. Gently press the dough into a thick rectangle about 6 by 4 inches (15 by 10 cm). Trim the edges even with a large sharp knife, then cut the dough into 6 equal squares.

Place the squares on the baking sheet, spacing them well apart. Bake until they are puffed and golden, 15–18 minutes. Transfer to a wire rack to cool slightly or completely.

Meanwhile, in a bowl, toss together the strawberries and the sugar with a fork, lightly crushing some of the berries. Cover the berries and refrigerate until well chilled or until serving time.

To serve, split the warm or cooled shortcakes in half horizontally and place the bottom halves, cut side up, on serving plates. Spoon some of the strawberries, including the juices, over each half and top with a dollop of the whipped cream. Top with the remaining shortcake halves, cut side down. Serve immediately.

MAKES 6 SERVINGS

FOR THE SHORTCAKES:

1⅔ cups (7½ oz/235 g) all-purpose (plain) flour

2 tablespoons sugar

1 tablespoon baking powder

1 teaspoon finely grated lemon zest

¾ teaspoon salt

½ cup (4 oz/125 g) cold unsalted butter, cut into small pieces

¾ cup (6 fl oz/180 ml) buttermilk

½ teaspoon vanilla extract (essence)

4 cups (1 lb/500 g) strawberries, hulled and cut into slices ¼ inch (6 mm) thick

¼ cup (1¾ oz/50 g) sugar

Sweetened Whipped Cream (page 113) for serving

LEMON CURD SQUARES

FOR THE CRUST:

1 cup (4½ oz/140 g) all-purpose (plain) flour

⅓ cup (2⅓ oz/70 g) granulated sugar

½ teaspoon salt

⅛ teaspoon ground cinnamon

½ cup (4 oz/125 g) cold unsalted butter, cut into ½-inch (12-mm) pieces, plus extra for greasing

FOR THE FILLING:

¾ cup (5¼ oz/160 g) granulated sugar

2 tablespoons all-purpose (plain) flour

Pinch of salt

1 teaspoon finely grated lemon zest (optional)

3 large eggs, at room temperature

½ cup (4 fl oz/125 ml) fresh lemon juice

3 tablespoons heavy (double) cream

Confectioners' (icing) sugar for dusting (optional)

To make the crust, preheat the oven to 350°F (180°C). Lightly grease an 8-inch (20-cm) square baking dish, preferably glass.

In a food processor, combine the flour, sugar, salt, and cinnamon. Pulse briefly until blended. Add the butter pieces and pulse until the dough forms moist crumbs and sticks together when pinched, about 1 minute. There should be no trace of dryness. Press the dough into the bottom and 1 inch (2.5 cm) up the sides of the prepared baking dish, lightly flouring your fingertips if necessary to prevent them from sticking. Bake the crust until pale golden, 20–22 minutes. Let the crust cool completely on a rack. Reduce the oven temperature to 325°F (165°C).

To make the filling, whisk together the sugar, flour, salt, and zest, if using. Add the eggs, lemon juice, and cream and whisk until just blended. Carefully pour the mixture over the baked crust.

Bake until the filling is set but still jiggles slightly when the dish is gently shaken, about 20 minutes, or longer if using a metal pan. Let cool on a rack for about 30 minutes. Run the tip of a small knife along the inside of the dish to loosen the crust from the sides, then let cool completely.

Cut into 12 small rectangles and carefully remove from the dish with a spatula. Sift a dusting of confectioners' sugar over the rectangles just before serving.

MAKES 12 BAR COOKIES

ZESTING AND JUICING

When zesting and juicing a lemon, always zest first. Use a zester or grater and make short, sweeping strokes, rotating the fruit slightly after every 1 or 2 swipes. Avoid removing the white pith, which imparts bitterness. To extract the most juice, press and roll the lemon on the countertop to crush it slightly, then halve it crosswise. For small amounts of juice, use a hand reamer or juicer, rotating the lemon and pressing and squeezing, until all the juice is released. For large amounts, electric juicers are efficient, but use caution, as they may "oversqueeze" and extract bitter pith.

ESPRESSO GRANITA

Place a 9-by-13-inch (23-by-33-cm) nonaluminum metal baking pan or glass baking dish in the freezer.

In a bowl, stir the sugar into the hot espresso until dissolved. Refrigerate until cool.

Pour the cooled espresso into the baking pan in the freezer. Freeze until crystals begin to form around the edges, about 30 minutes. Using a fork, stir and scrape around the edges and in the corners to evenly distribute the crystals. Freeze for another 30 minutes and stir and scrape again, breaking up any large crystals as they form. Continue freezing and stirring every 30 minutes until the entire contents of the pan have crystallized, 3–4 hours total. Cover and keep frozen until ready to serve.

Spoon into individual glasses or bowls and garnish each serving with a dollop of whipped cream and, if desired, a sprinkling of ground cinnamon.

Variation Tip: For a Latte Granita, add 1 cup (8 fl oz/250 ml) whole milk after dissolving the sugar in the hot espresso and proceed as directed.

MAKES 8-10 SERVINGS

⅔ cup (4⅔ oz/145 g) sugar

4 cups (32 fl oz/1 l) hot brewed espresso or double-strength brewed coffee

Sweetened Whipped Cream (page 113) for garnish

Ground cinnamon for garnish (optional)

ABOUT COFFEE BEANS
The most important factor in making good coffee or espresso is the coffee bean. Select whole beans freshly roasted to your liking. For espresso, use a darker Italian or French roast. Buy in small quantities and, if you have a grinder at home, do not grind the beans at the store, as the flavor begins to diminish the moment the beans are ground. Store unused whole beans in a cool, dry, dark place. Freshly roasted beans will keep well for about a week. In a pinch, put them in the freezer, but expect some loss of flavor.

SUMMER FRUIT DESSERTS

The following recipes play up the natural sweetness of summer fruits without overpowering their flavors. When sultry weather arrives, turn to a rich old-fashioned ice cream or delicate sorbet for sweet relief. Whether serving up a picnic treat or a homey ending to a family barbecue, you'll enjoy these easy desserts throughout the lazy months.

BLUEBERRY TURNOVERS

Preheat the oven to 400°F (200°C). Line the bottom of a rimmed baking sheet with parchment (baking) paper.

In a bowl, toss the blueberries with the brown sugar, flour, lemon juice, vanilla, zest, and salt, crushing the berries slightly with the back of a spoon, until the dry ingredients are evenly moist. Set the mixture aside.

In a small bowl, using a fork, make an egg wash by stirring together the egg and water until well blended. Set aside.

On a lightly floured work surface, roll out one dough disk into a 10½-inch (27-cm) square about ⅛ inch (3 mm) thick. Use a dough scraper or an icing spatula to loosen the pastry if it sticks. Trim away the ragged edges, removing about ¼ inch (6 mm) from each side. Repeat with the second disk. Cut each square into four 5-inch (13-cm) squares.

Spoon some of the blueberry filling onto the center of each square, dividing the filling evenly. Lightly brush the edges of the squares with some of the egg wash, then fold the dough over the filling to form triangles. Crimp the edges with the tines of a fork to seal. Place on the prepared baking sheet about 1½ inches (4 cm) apart. Brush the turnovers with the remaining egg wash and sprinkle evenly with the almonds and granulated sugar, if desired. Cut 2 or 3 small slits in the top of each turnover to vent.

Bake the turnovers until golden, 20–25 minutes. Let cool on a rack. Serve warm or at room temperature.

MAKES 8 TURNOVERS

EGG WASH

These turnovers, like many double-crust pies, are brushed with an egg wash before baking. The wash, a mixture of egg or egg yolk and water, milk, or cream beaten together until just blended, gives the baked crust a lovely golden color. Use a pastry brush to swab the dough lightly but evenly. The egg wash also helps to hold on toppings like the sugar or almonds used here.

1¼ cups (5 oz/155 g) blueberries

2 tablespoons firmly packed light brown sugar

1 tablespoon all-purpose (plain) flour

1 teaspoon fresh lemon juice

½ teaspoon vanilla extract (essence)

¼ teaspoon finely grated lemon zest

Pinch of salt

1 large egg, at room temperature

2 teaspoons water

Double recipe Basic Pastry Dough (page 113), divided into 2 equal disks and chilled

2 tablespoons sliced (flaked) almonds (optional)

2 teaspoons granulated sugar (optional)

BLACKBERRY COBBLER

Unsalted butter for greasing

FOR THE FILLING:

6 cups (1½ lb/750 g) blackberries

⅓ cup (2⅓ oz/70 g) sugar

1 tablespoon all-purpose (plain) flour

1 teaspoon finely grated lemon zest

Pinch of salt

FOR THE TOPPING:

1¼ cups (5¾ oz/175 g) all-purpose (plain) flour

⅓ cup (2⅓ oz/70 g) sugar

2 teaspoons baking powder

½ teaspoon ground cinnamon

¼ teaspoon salt

1 large egg, at room temperature

½ cup (4 fl oz/125 ml) buttermilk

6 tablespoons (3 oz/90 g) unsalted butter, melted and cooled slightly

½ teaspoon vanilla extract (essence)

Preheat the oven to 375°F (190°C). Lightly grease a 2-qt (2-l) oval or round baking dish.

To make the filling, gently toss the blackberries with the sugar, flour, zest, and salt in a large bowl until blended. Pour into the prepared baking dish and set aside.

To make the topping, stir together the flour, sugar, baking powder, cinnamon, and salt in a bowl. In another bowl, whisk together the egg, buttermilk, melted butter, and vanilla until well blended. Pour the wet ingredients into the dry ingredients and, using a rubber spatula, fold gently until the flour is moistened and the mixture forms a soft dough.

Drop heaping spoonfuls of the mixture onto the fruit, spacing them evenly over the surface. The topping will not completely cover the fruit. Bake until the fruit filling is bubbling, the topping is browned, and a toothpick inserted into the topping comes out clean, about 45 minutes. Serve warm or at room temperature.

MAKES 8–10 SERVINGS

COBBLER VARIATIONS

For another version of this cobbler, try mixing some raspberries and blueberries in with the blackberries. Or, replace the blackberries altogether with sliced peaches or nectarines and a handful of dried sour cherries or cranberries. A combination of 3 or 4 plum varieties, all pitted and quartered, is also wonderful. Add a pinch of freshly grated nutmeg or a dash of vanilla or almond extract (essence) to the fruit. Or, sprinkle a small handful of sliced (flaked) almonds or chopped pecans over the topping before baking.

PEACH ICE CREAM

Bring a saucepan three-fourths full of water to a boil. Cut a shallow X on the blossom end of the three peaches. Immerse them in the boiling water for 30 seconds. Using a slotted spoon, transfer to a work surface. When cool enough to handle, slip off the skins, using your fingertips or a small, sharp knife. Remove the pits and finely chop the peaches, capturing their juices. Put the peaches and juices in a small bowl and add the 2 tablespoons sugar and the lemon juice. Toss together and set aside, stirring occasionally.

In a saucepan over medium heat, warm the milk and cream until small bubbles appear along the edge of the pan. Remove from the heat. In a bowl, whisk together the egg yolks and the ⅓ cup sugar until pale and thick. Slowly pour the hot milk mixture into the eggs while whisking. Whisk until well blended. Return the mixture to the saucepan over medium-low heat. Cook, stirring constantly, until the custard is thickened enough to coat the back of a spoon, about 4 minutes. Pour through a sieve set over a clean bowl. Stir any accumulated juices from the peaches into the custard. Cover and refrigerate, stirring frequently, until very cold, about 2 hours. To speed the process, use an ice bath (page 66).

Set a bowl in the freezer to hold the finished ice cream. Add the vanilla and salt to the chilled custard and stir well, then pour into an ice-cream maker and freeze according to the manufacturer's instructions. When the ice cream is ready, spoon it into the chilled bowl. Add the chopped peaches and any additional juices and stir gently to distribute evenly. Freeze until ready to serve or up to overnight. Spoon into dessert bowls and garnish with the peach slices, if desired.

MAKES ABOUT 3 CUPS (24 FL OZ/750 ML), OR 6 SERVINGS

3 large, ripe peaches, plus 1 peach, sliced, for garnish (optional)

⅓ cup (2⅓ oz/70 g) plus 2 tablespoons sugar

2 teaspoons fresh lemon juice

1⅓ cups (11 fl oz/340 ml) whole milk

⅔ cup (5 fl oz/160 ml) heavy (double) cream

6 large egg yolks

1 teaspoon vanilla extract (essence)

Pinch of salt

CHERRY CLAFOUTIS

Unsalted butter for greasing

¾ lb (375 g) sweet cherries, pitted and halved

3 tablespoons dark rum

¼ cup (1⅛ oz/34 g) all-purpose (plain) flour

½ cup (3½ oz/105 g) sugar, plus extra for dusting

¼ teaspoon salt

3 large eggs, at room temperature

1 cup (8 fl oz/250 ml) heavy (double) cream

Preheat the oven to 375°F (190°C). Grease a shallow 9-by-14-inch (23-by-35-cm) baking dish with a 2-qt (2-l) capacity and dust with sugar. Tap out any excess.

In a small bowl, toss together the cherries and rum and set aside.

In another bowl, whisk together the flour, sugar, and salt. Add the eggs and whisk until the batter is smooth. Slowly pour in the cream, whisking constantly. Stir the cherries and their juices into the batter until just blended. Pour the batter into the prepared baking dish.

Bake until puffed and golden, 33–35 minutes. Serve hot and puffed, or let cool to room temperature on a rack before serving. The clafoutis will deflate as it cools, but will still be delicious.

MAKES 6–8 SERVINGS

CHERRY VARIETIES

Cherries are either sweet or sour. The sour ones, used for pies and jams, are seldom sold fresh. Sweet cherries are the ones everyone clamors for when they first appear in early summer. The sweet Bing is the deep red-black cherry most often seen, while the Rainier, widely considered the sweetest, is a bright red and sometimes gold cherry (above). Both are delicious and are just two of the many varieties available. Although traditional clafoutis is made with unpitted whole cherries, said to add extra cherry flavor, this luscious pit-free version does not lack for flavor but is a little easier to eat.

FIG GALETTE

PLEATING THE DOUGH

To make this rustic galette, the outer edge of a dough round is folded over fruit and then loosely pleated. To form the pleats, using both hands, lift the edge of the dough up and over the fruit and then fold it underneath itself every 1–2 inches (2.5–5 cm) until the entire edge is a series of loose folds. Work the dough quickly with cold hands. If you linger, the heat from your fingers will melt the butter in the dough, resulting in a tougher crust. To cool your hands before you begin, run them under very cold water and then dry them well.

Preheat the oven to 400°F (200°C). Line a rimmed baking sheet with parchment (baking) paper.

Lightly dust a work surface and a rolling pin with flour. Roll out the chilled pastry dough into a round slightly larger than 13 inches (33 cm) and about ⅛ inch (3 mm) thick. Lift and turn the dough several times as you roll to prevent sticking, and dust the surface and the rolling pin with additional flour as needed. Use a dough scraper or an icing spatula to loosen the pastry if it sticks. Trim off any ragged edges to make an even 13-inch (33-cm) round. Cover with plastic wrap and set aside.

In a large bowl, gently toss together the figs, brown sugar, zest, and vanilla until all the ingredients are evenly distributed. Uncover the dough and transfer to the baking sheet. The edges of the dough round will hang over the pan edges. Arrange the figs in a pile in the center of the dough, leaving a 2-inch (5-cm) border uncovered. Fold the dough up and over the filling, pleating loosely all around the circle and leaving the galette open in center *(left)*. Brush the pleated dough with the cream. Sprinkle the almonds on top of the dough and press on them lightly to help them stick.

Bake until the crust is golden and the figs are tender when pierced with the tip of a knife, about 40 minutes. Let cool on a rack. Serve warm or at room temperature.

MAKES 6-8 SERVINGS

Basic Pastry Dough (page 113), chilled

1¼ lb (625 g) ripe fresh figs, stemmed and quartered lengthwise

⅓ cup (2½ oz/75 g) firmly packed brown sugar

1½ teaspoons finely grated lemon zest

1 teaspoon vanilla extract (essence)

2 tablespoons heavy (double) cream or whole milk

¼ cup (1 oz/30 g) sliced (flaked) almonds

MANGO SORBET

¾ cup (6 fl oz / 180 ml) water

½ cup (3½ oz / 105 g) sugar

3 ripe mangoes

2 tablespoons fresh lemon juice

1 teaspoon finely grated lime zest, plus longer zest strips for optional garnish

Pinch of salt

Place a container in the freezer to hold the finished sorbet.

In a small saucepan over medium-high heat, combine the water and sugar. Bring to a boil, stirring frequently until the sugar dissolves. When the liquid boils, remove from the heat and set aside to cool.

Meanwhile, cut the flesh of each mango away from its pit, score the flesh in chunks, and then cut the chunks from the skin *(right)*. Put the mango pieces in a food processor and process until smooth. Measure out 1½ cups (12 fl oz / 375 ml) mango purée and stir it into the cooled sugar syrup along with the lemon juice, lime zest, and salt. Stir until well blended.

Freeze the mango mixture in an ice-cream maker according to the manufacturer's instructions. Spoon into the chilled container, cover, and freeze until ready to serve or for up to 2 days. Spoon into individual glasses or bowls and, if desired, garnish with the zest strips.

MAKES 6 SERVINGS

PREPARING MANGO

Hold a mango on one of its narrow sides on a cutting board. Using a sharp knife set just off center to avoid the pit, slice lengthwise to remove one side of the mango in one piece. Repeat with the other side. One at a time, place a mango half cut side up on a cutting board and carefully score the flesh in a crosshatch pattern, cutting down to, but not through, the skin. Then, with the cut side up, press against the skin with your thumbs, forcing the cubes upward. Cut across the bottom of the cubes, freeing them from the skin.

SUMMER FRUIT COMPOTE

To make the dressing, in a small saucepan over medium heat, combine the lime juice, honey, orange and lime zests, ginger, salt, and cayenne, if using. Whisk until warm and well blended. Remove from the heat and set aside.

Using a melon baller, scoop out the melon flesh and place it in a large bowl. Slice the plums and nectarine lengthwise into wedges ½ inch (12 mm) wide. Add them to the bowl with the melon balls. Cut the kiwifruit flesh lengthwise into quarters, and then cut the quarters crosswise into chunks 1 inch (2.5 cm) wide. Add to the bowl. Finally, cut the strawberries lengthwise into quarters and add them to the bowl, along with the whole blueberries.

Drizzle the dressing over the fruit. Toss gently to combine. Cover and refrigerate until chilled, at least 1 hour or up to 6 hours. Just before serving, add the mint and toss to combine.

MAKES 8 SERVINGS

SHREDDING HERBS

There's a trick to making the thin strips of fresh herbs, called a chiffonade, sometimes asked for in dessert recipes. Pick off large fresh mint leaves from 1 or more fresh sprigs. Try to use same-sized leaves and preferably larger ones, which are easier to manage.

Stack the leaves on the work surface and roll them up lengthwise like a cigar. Hold the roll of leaves with your fingertips to keep it tight, then cut the roll crosswise into very thin shreds with a sharp knife.

FOR THE DRESSING:

¼ cup (2 fl oz/60 ml) fresh lime juice

¼ cup (2 fl oz/60 ml) honey

1 teaspoon finely grated orange zest

1 teaspoon finely grated lime zest

½ teaspoon peeled and finely grated fresh ginger

Pinch of salt

Pinch of cayenne pepper (optional)

½ small honeydew melon, seeded

2 plums, pitted

1 nectarine or peach, pitted

1 kiwifruit, peeled

2 cups (8 oz/250 g) strawberries, stems removed

1 cup (4 oz/125 g) blueberries

⅓ cup (½ oz/15 g) finely shredded fresh mint leaves *(far left)*

HOLIDAY DESSERTS

Whether prepared for a family meal or a party, a homemade dessert at holiday time is always special. The recipes that follow range from simple to elaborate, allowing you to choose as time permits during this busy season. From an old-fashioned apple pie to a homey spiced gingerbread to a classic bûche de Noël, these do-ahead desserts are a fitting end to a holiday feast.

PUMPKIN PIE

FLUTING PIE DOUGH

To create a decorative fluted edge for a pie crust, hold the index finger of one hand on the inside of the rim of the crust and the index finger and thumb of the other hand on the outside rim. Pinch with the thumb and index finger of the outside hand while pressing in between them with the index finger of the other. Repeat around the entire edge. For a rope edge, position the thumb at an angle on the inside rim of the crust, and place the index finger of the same hand on the opposite outside edge. Press the pastry toward the thumb with the finger, working around the entire edge.

Lightly dust a work surface and a rolling pin with flour. Roll out the chilled dough into a 14-inch (35-cm) round about ⅛ inch (3 mm) thick. Lift and turn the dough several times as you roll to prevent sticking, and dust the surface and the rolling pin with additional flour as needed. Use a dough scraper or icing spatula to loosen the pastry round if it sticks.

Carefully roll the dough around the pin and position it over a 9-inch (23-cm) pie plate, preferably glass. Unroll the dough and fit it into the plate, gently but firmly pressing the dough against the sides and bottom while taking care not to pull or stretch it. Trim the edges, leaving a ¾-inch (2-cm) overhang. Roll the overhang under itself to create a high edge on the plate's rim. Flute the edge decoratively *(left)* and freeze for at least 30 minutes.

Preheat the oven to 425°F (220°C). Line the frozen crust with aluminum foil and fill with pie weights, uncooked rice, or dried beans. Bake for 15 minutes. Remove the weights and foil and continue to bake until the shell is golden, 4–5 minutes longer. Let the shell cool completely on a rack. Reduce the oven temperature to 325°F (165°C).

In a large bowl, combine the pumpkin purée, brown sugar, cream, whole eggs and egg yolk, flour, vanilla, cinnamon, nutmeg, cloves, and salt and whisk until smooth. Pour into the crust.

Bake the pie until the filling is set but the center still jiggles slightly when the pie plate is gently shaken, about 50 minutes, or longer if using a metal pie pan. Let cool completely on a rack. Serve at room temperature or slightly chilled, topping with the whipped cream, if desired.

MAKES ONE 9-INCH (23-CM) PIE, OR 10 SERVINGS

Basic Pastry Dough (page 113), chilled

1 can (15 oz/470 g) pumpkin purée

⅔ cup (5⅓ oz/165 g) firmly packed light brown sugar

1 cup (8 fl oz/250 ml) heavy (double) cream

2 whole large eggs, plus 1 large egg yolk, at room temperature

4 teaspoons all-purpose (plain) flour

⅔ teaspoon vanilla extract (essence)

⅔ teaspoon ground cinnamon

¼ teaspoon freshly grated nutmeg

Pinch of ground cloves

Pinch of salt

Sweetened Whipped Cream (page 113) for serving (optional)

APPLE PIE WITH CHEDDAR CHEESE

Double recipe Basic Pastry Dough (page 113), divided into 2 disks and chilled

3 lb (1.5 kg) baking apples (page 13), peeled, cored, and cut lengthwise into slices a scant ¼ inch (6 mm) thick

⅔ cup (5⅓ oz/165 g) firmly packed dark brown sugar

3 tablespoons all-purpose (plain) flour

1¼ teaspoons ground cinnamon

¼ teaspoon freshly grated nutmeg

Pinch of ground cloves

1 teaspoon vanilla extract (essence)

1 teaspoon finely grated orange zest

Pinch of salt

8–10 thick slices extra-sharp Cheddar cheese

Preheat the oven to 425°F (220°C). Line a rimmed baking sheet with aluminum foil.

Lightly dust a work surface and a rolling pin with flour. Roll out one disk of chilled dough into a 14-inch (35-cm) round about ⅛ inch (3 mm) thick. Lift and turn the dough several times as you roll to prevent sticking, and dust the surface and the rolling pin with additional flour as needed. Use a dough scraper or an icing spatula to loosen the pastry round if it sticks.

Carefully roll the dough around the pin and position over a 9-inch (23-cm) glass pie dish. Unroll the dough and fit it into the dish, gently but firmly pressing the dough against the sides and bottom while taking care not to stretch it. Leave the excess hanging over the sides and cover the pie dish with plastic wrap. Roll out the other disk to a 14-inch circle and cover with plastic wrap.

In a large bowl, combine the apples, brown sugar, flour, cinnamon, nutmeg, cloves, vanilla, zest, and salt. Toss until well blended.

Uncover the pie doughs. Mound the apple filling, along with any accumulated juices, in the pastry-lined pie dish. Brush the dough around the edge of the dish with water. Roll the top crust around the pin and position it over the pie. Unroll it, centering the dough over the filling. Press the edges of the dough rounds together, trim the overhang to ½ inch (12 mm), roll the overhang under itself to create a high edge on the dish's rim, and crimp to seal the edges *(right)*. With a paring knife, cut 3 vent holes in the top crust.

Set the pie on the foil-lined sheet. Bake for 15 minutes. Reduce the heat to 350°F (180°C) and continue to bake until the apples are very tender when pierced through a vent with a knife and the crust is golden, about 50 minutes longer. Let cool on a rack. Serve warm or at room temperature with slices of Cheddar cheese.

MAKES ONE 9-INCH (23-CM) PIE, OR 8-10 SERVINGS

CRIMPING PIE DOUGH

The crusts of a double-crust pie must be crimped together to hold in the filling. Once the bottom crust is filled, brush the rim of the dough with water. Roll the top crust around the pin and position it over the pie. Gently unroll it, centering the dough over the filling. Press the edges together and, with kitchen scissors, trim the crust to leave a ½-inch (12-mm) overhang. Roll the dough underneath itself to shape a high edge resting on the dish rim. Crimp to seal the edges, pressing down with the tines of a fork around the entire edge of the crust.

PECAN TART

Lightly dust a work surface and a rolling pin with flour. Roll out the chilled dough into a 13-inch (33-cm) round about ⅛ inch (3 mm) thick. Lift and turn the dough several times as you roll to prevent sticking, and dust the surface and the rolling pin with additional flour as needed. Use a dough scraper or icing spatula to loosen the pastry round if it sticks.

Carefully roll the dough around the pin and position it over a 9½-inch (24-cm) tart pan with a removable bottom. Unroll the dough and fit it into the pan, gently but firmly pressing the dough against the sides and bottom while taking care not to pull or stretch it. Trim the edges, leaving a ½-inch (12-mm) overhang. Fold the overhang back over itself and press it into the sides of the pan, creating a double thickness to reinforce the sides of the tart shell. Freeze until the shell is firm, at least 30 minutes.

Preheat the oven to 425°F (220°C). Line the frozen shell with aluminum foil and fill with pie weights, uncooked rice, or dried beans. Bake for 15 minutes. Remove the weights and foil and continue to bake until the shell is pale golden, 4–5 minutes longer. Let the shell cool completely on a rack. Reduce the oven temperature to 350°F (180°C).

In a bowl, combine the eggs, corn syrup, brown sugar, melted butter, vanilla, and salt. Whisk until blended. Scatter the toasted nuts evenly in the cooled tart shell. Carefully pour the egg mixture evenly over the nuts, being careful not to disturb them.

Bake until the filling is set and slightly puffed and the center still jiggles slightly when the pan is gently shaken, about 30 minutes. Let cool on a rack. Serve warm or at room temperature, topped with whipped cream, if desired.

MAKES ONE 9½-INCH (24-CM) TART, OR 8 SERVINGS

Basic Pastry Dough (page 113), chilled

3 large eggs, at room temperature

¾ cup (7½ fl oz/235 ml) light corn syrup

½ cup (4 oz/125 g) firmly packed light brown sugar

3 tablespoons unsalted butter, melted and slightly cooled

1 teaspoon vanilla extract (essence)

Pinch of salt

1⅓ cups (5½ oz/170 g) chopped pecans, toasted (page 115)

Sweetened Whipped Cream (page 113) for serving (optional)

GINGERBREAD

1²/₃ cups (7½ oz/235 g) all-purpose (plain) flour, plus extra for dusting

¾ teaspoon baking powder

¼ teaspoon baking soda (bicarbonate of soda)

1½ teaspoons ground ginger

1 teaspoon ground cinnamon

¼ teaspoon freshly grated nutmeg

¼ teaspoon salt

6 tablespoons (3 oz/90 g) unsalted butter, at room temperature, plus extra for greasing

½ cup (4 oz/125 g) firmly packed dark brown sugar

2 large eggs, at room temperature

1 teaspoon finely grated orange zest (optional)

½ cup (5½ oz/170 g) light molasses

½ cup (4 fl oz/125 ml) warm water

Sweetened Whipped Cream (page 113) for serving

Preheat the oven to 350°F (180°C). Lightly grease an 8-inch (20-cm) square baking dish and dust with flour.

In a bowl, whisk together the flour, baking powder, baking soda, ginger, cinnamon, nutmeg, and salt until well blended. Set aside. In another bowl, using a mixer on medium speed, beat together the butter and brown sugar until well blended and fluffy. Add the eggs one at a time, beating well after each addition, until just blended. Add the zest, if using, and beat until blended. Continue beating while slowly adding the molasses. Sprinkle the flour mixture over the egg mixture and stir until just incorporated. Add the water and stir until blended. Pour into the prepared pan and spread evenly.

Bake until the gingerbread is puffed and a toothpick inserted into the center comes out clean, about 35 minutes. Let cool on a rack. Cut into squares and serve warm or at room temperature with a dollop of whipped cream.

MAKES ONE 8-INCH (20-CM) SQUARE CAKE, OR 9 SERVINGS

MOLASSES STYLES

Thick molasses is a by-product of sugar cane processing. After the sugar has crystallized, the remaining syrup is refined in three stages, or boilings. The first results in light molasses, which is dark, very sweet, and smooth. The next boiling yields dark molasses, which is darker and less sweet than the light. The third and final boiling produces the very thick and bitter-tasting blackstrap. Almost all molasses sold today is unsulfured. Sulfur was once regularly added to help clarify the cane liquids during sugar processing, but its use has largely ended because of a high incidence of allergic reaction.

BÛCHE DE NOËL

USING AN ICE BATH
To cool a mixture down more rapidly than by simple refrigeration, set it in an ice bath. Fill a bowl larger than the one holding the mixture about one-third full of ice. Add about 1 cup (8 fl oz/ 250 ml) water. Nestle the smaller bowl into the ice water. Adding the water to the ice makes the ice's chilling power much more effective. This same principle works for chilling wine: add water to an ice bucket to keep wine cold.

Preheat the oven to 350°F (180°C). Grease a 15½-by-10½-inch rimmed baking sheet and line the bottom with parchment (baking) paper. Grease and flour the paper and the pan sides.

To make the cake, whisk the flour, baking powder, and salt in a bowl until blended. In a large bowl, using a mixer on medium-high speed, beat the eggs until pale and thick, about 3 minutes. Add the granulated sugar and vanilla and continue beating until tripled in volume, about 3 minutes more. Sprinkle the flour mixture over the eggs and, using a rubber spatula, fold gently until just blended. Pour the batter into the prepared pan and spread evenly. Bake until the cake springs back when lightly touched, 13–15 minutes.

While the cake is baking, lay a clean kitchen towel on the counter and sift confectioners' sugar generously onto it, covering it evenly. When the cake is ready, remove it from the oven and immediately run a knife around the inside of the pan to loosen the cake. Holding the cake in place, invert the pan onto the prepared towel. Lift off the pan and carefully peel off the paper. Beginning on a long edge, roll up the cake and towel together. Set on a rack and let cool.

To make the syrup, combine the water and granulated sugar in a small saucepan over medium heat and stir until the sugar dissolves. Bring to a boil and remove from the heat. Stir in the rum and set aside to cool to room temperature.

To make the frosting, combine the chocolate and cream in the top of a double boiler (page 106). Set over barely simmering water and melt the chocolate, then whisk until well blended. Remove the bowl from the heat and refrigerate, stirring occasionally, until cold, about 2 hours. To speed this process, use an ice bath *(left)*. When the mixture is cold, add the vanilla and salt. Using a mixer on medium-high speed, beat the chocolate mixture briefly until firm enough to hold a soft dollop. The mixture will continue to firm up as it sits.

FOR THE CAKE:

Unsalted butter for greasing

1 cup (4½ oz/140 g) all-purpose (plain) flour, plus extra for dusting

¾ teaspoon baking powder

¼ teaspoon salt

4 large eggs, at room temperature

⅔ cup (4⅔ oz/145 g) granulated sugar

1¼ teaspoons vanilla extract (essence)

Confectioners' (icing) sugar for dusting

FOR THE SYRUP:

¼ cup (2 fl oz/60 ml) water

¼ cup (1¾ oz/50 g) granulated sugar

2–3 tablespoons dark rum or coffee-flavored liqueur

FOR THE FROSTING:

10 oz (315 g) bittersweet chocolate, finely chopped

2¼ cups (18 fl oz/560 ml) heavy (double) cream

1 teaspoon vanilla extract (essence)

Pinch of salt

MERINGUE MUSHROOMS

FOR THE MERINGUE:

3 large egg whites, at room temperature

¼ teaspoon cream of tartar

½ cup (3½ oz/105 g) granulated sugar

⅓ cup (1⅓ oz/40 g) confectioners' (icing) sugar

Unsweetened cocoa powder for dusting

Chocolate curls for garnish (page 105)

Confectioners' (icing) sugar for garnish

Preheat the oven to 225°F (110°C). Line 2 baking sheets with parchment. Have ready a pastry bag fitted with a small (no. 6) plain tip. In a bowl, using a mixer on medium-low speed, beat together the egg whites and cream of tartar until very foamy. Slowly add the granulated sugar while beating. Increase the speed to high and beat until soft peaks form when the beaters are lifted. Continue until the whites hold stiff, shiny peaks. Sift the confectioners' sugar over the whites and, using a rubber spatula, fold in until well blended.

Scoop the mixture into the bag. On 1 baking sheet, pipe 48 stems, each ½ inch (12 mm) wide at the base and tapering off to a point at the top, ¾ inch (2 cm) tall, and spaced about ½ inch (12 mm) apart. On the other sheet, pipe 48 mounds for the tops, each about 1¼ inches (3 cm) wide and ¾ inch (2 cm) high, also spaced ½ inch (12 mm) apart. With a damp fingertip, gently smooth any pointy tips. Dust with cocoa. Reserve the remaining meringue.

Bake until dry and firm enough to lift off the paper, 50–55 minutes. Set the pans on the counter and turn the mounds flat side up. With the tip of a knife, carefully make a small hole in the flat side of each mound. Pipe small dabs of the remaining meringue into the holes and insert the stems tip first. Return to the oven until completely dry, about 15 minutes longer. Let cool completely on the sheets.

To assemble the *bûche*, unroll the cake and brush it liberally with the cooled syrup. Using an icing spatula, spread one-third of the frosting over the cake. Gently reroll the cake and place, seam side down, on a cutting board. Frost the top and sides of the roll with the remaining frosting, using long, rough strokes. Using a serrated knife, trim each end on a sharp angle. Transfer to a serving plate and garnish with the chocolate curls, a sifting of confectioners' sugar, and the meringue mushrooms. Pass the remaining meringue mushrooms at the table for garnishing individual servings.

MAKES 12–16 SERVINGS   *(Photograph appears on following page.)*

BEATING EGG WHITES

To beat egg whites into glossy billows, start with a spotlessly clean bowl and beaters. Start beating the whites on medium-low speed. Add cream of tartar, to help stabilize the foam, and increase the speed of the mixer. (If you are using a copper bowl, which naturally stabilizes egg whites, omit the cream of tartar.) When the whites are soft and foamy but still loose, begin slowly adding the sugar. The whites will grow thick and shiny as you continue beating. To test the degree of stiffness, lift the beaters. The peaks on the beaters' tips fall gently to one side when soft and will hold their shape when stiff.

POACHED PEARS WITH RASPBERRY COULIS

CORING WHOLE PEARS
Recipes often call for peeling and coring pears whole, leaving the stem end intact. Use a small, sharp knife for peeling, and immediately brush the fruit with lemon juice to keep the flesh from darkening upon exposure to the air. A variety of tools can be used for coring: a small spoon with a sharp-edged bowl such as a grapefruit spoon, the large end of a melon baller, or an apple corer. Working from the blossom end of the pear, scoop out the seeds and the membrane, being careful to stop within ½ inch (12 mm) of the pear's stem end.

Peel the pears and generously rub with the lemon half to prevent discoloring. Working from the blossom end, core each pear, leaving the stem end intact (*left*). Squeeze a little juice from the lemon half into each cavity.

Select a deep saucepan with a tight-fitting lid just large enough to accommodate the pears. Combine the orange juice, water, sugar, lemon and orange zests, vanilla bean, clove, peppercorns, and salt in the saucepan and place over medium-high heat. Bring to a boil, stirring to dissolve the sugar. When a boil is reached, reduce the heat to medium-low and add the peeled pears. Place a round of parchment (baking) paper cut to fit the diameter of the pan directly on the liquid and pears. Cover with the lid and simmer gently until the pears are just tender when pierced with a knife, 12–18 minutes. The timing depends on the ripeness and size of the fruit. For even cooking, adjust the pears' positions several times during poaching. Remove from the heat and let the pears cool completely in the liquid.

Using a slotted spoon, transfer the pears to a bowl and set aside. Pick out the zests, clove, and peppercorns from the syrup and discard, then pick out the vanilla bean and, using the tip of a knife, scrape its seeds back into the pan. Bring the liquid to a boil over high heat and cook until thickened and syrupy, 3–5 minutes. Pour the syrup over the pears, cover the bowl, and refrigerate.

Serve the pears, slightly chilled, in a pool of raspberry coulis and drizzled with a little syrup.

Note: Bosc or Bartlett (Williams') pears are good choices for this dish.

MAKES 4 SERVINGS

4 small, firm yet ripe pears (see Note)

½ lemon

2½ cups (20 fl oz/625 ml) fresh orange juice

2½ cups (20 fl oz/625 ml) water

⅔ cup (4⅔ oz/145 g) sugar

3 lemon zest strips

3 orange zest strips

½ vanilla bean, split lengthwise

1 whole clove

4 peppercorns

Pinch of salt

Raspberry Coulis (page 113) for serving

STEAMED PERSIMMON PUDDING

¾ cup (3–4 oz/90–125 g) mixed dried fruit such as chopped apricots and whole golden raisins (sultanas) and cranberries

¼ cup (2 fl oz/60 ml) brandy

¾ cup (3¼ oz/95 g) all-purpose (plain) flour

¾ teaspoon ground cinnamon

½ teaspoon ground ginger

¼ teaspoon salt

Pinch of ground cloves

1 egg, at room temperature

⅔ cup (5⅓ oz/165 g) firmly packed light brown sugar

⅔ cup (5 fl oz/160 ml) Hachiya persimmon purée, at room temperature *(far right)*

½ cup (4 oz/125 g) unsalted butter, melted and cooled, plus extra for greasing

1½ teaspoons vanilla extract (essence)

1 teaspoon finely grated orange zest

2 tablespoons hot water

1 teaspoon baking soda (bicarbonate of soda)

Boiling water as needed

Sweetened Whipped Cream (page 113) for serving

In a small saucepan, stir together the dried fruit and brandy. Bring to a boil over medium heat, cover, and remove from the heat. Let stand, stirring occasionally, until the fruit is plumped, 20 minutes.

Generously butter a 5- or 6-cup (40– or 48–fl oz/1.25- or 1.5-l) pudding mold with a lid and a piece of aluminum foil large enough to cover the top of the mold. Choose a saucepan with a tight-fitting lid deep enough to contain the mold and a wire cooling rack. Place the rack in the bottom of the pan and add water to just cover the rack. The water should be about 1 inch (2.5 cm) deep. Set aside.

In a bowl, whisk together the flour, cinnamon, ginger, salt, and cloves. In a large bowl, beat together the egg and brown sugar until well blended. Add the persimmon purée, melted butter, vanilla, and orange zest and beat until well blended. In a small bowl, stir together the hot water and the baking soda. Add to the persimmon mixture and stir until well blended. Sprinkle the flour mixture over the persimmon mixture and stir just until blended. Fold in the plumped dried fruit and any remaining brandy.

Pour the mixture into the prepared mold, smoothing the surface. Cover with the buttered foil, buttered side down, and snap on the mold lid. Set the mold on the rack in the pan, cover the pan, and bring the water to a boil. Reduce the heat to low or medium-low and simmer vigorously until the pudding is firm when the top is pressed, about 1¼ hours. Check the water level every 30 minutes or so and add boiling water as needed to maintain the level.

Carefully transfer the mold to a rack and let cool until it can be handled, about 15 minutes. Remove the lid and foil. Invert the mold onto a flat serving plate and carefully lift off the mold. Using a serrated knife, cut into slices while still warm. Let cool to room temperature if desired, and serve with the whipped cream.

MAKES 8 SERVINGS

ABOUT PERSIMMONS
Fuyu and Hachiya are the two most common varieties of persimmon. The Fuyu is firm and crunchy when ripe, while the Hachiya, shaped like a large acorn with a dry, brown leafy top, is quite soft when ripe. Eaten too early, it has a harsh and astringent flavor. For this recipe, choose 2 or 3 Hachiya persimmons that are bright orange with stem leaves attached and that yield easily when pressed with your fingertip. Cut away the top and scoop out the pulp. Process briefly in a food processor, then press through a sieve to remove any stringy fibers.

SPECIAL OCCASIONS

No matter what the occasion—a birthday, an anniversary, a fancy dinner party, a college graduation—celebrate it in style with a showstopping dessert. The recipes in this chapter aren't difficult, but they've got personality. Choose from among frozen, flaming, layered, and classic—every one of them memorable, as pretty to present as it is delicious to eat.

CLASSIC BIRTHDAY CAKE

Preheat the oven to 350°F (180°C). Lightly grease the bottoms of two 9-by-2-inch (23-by-5-cm) round cake pans and line with parchment (baking) paper. Lightly grease the paper and sides of the pans with butter and dust with flour. In a bowl, whisk together the flour, baking powder, and salt until well blended. In another bowl, using a mixer on medium speed, beat the butter until smooth. Slowly add the granulated sugar and continue beating until well blended and fluffy. Add the eggs one at a time, beating well after each addition, until just blended. Beat in the vanilla. Add the flour mixture in 3 batches alternately with the buttermilk in 2 batches, beating on low speed after each addition.

Divide the batter between the prepared pans and spread evenly. Bake until a toothpick inserted into the center of a cake comes out clean, 25–30 minutes. Let cool on a rack for 15 minutes. Run a small knife around the inside of each pan to loosen the cake. Invert onto the rack and lift off the pans. Carefully peel off the parchment paper, then let the layers cool completely before frosting.

To make the frosting, combine the chocolates in the top of a double boiler (page 106). Set over barely simmering water and stir until melted. Let cool slightly. In a large bowl, using a mixer on medium speed, beat together the butter and confectioners' sugar until fluffy. Beat in the corn syrup, vanilla, and salt. Continue beating while gradually adding the chocolate. Beat until smooth.

To assemble, brush away any loose crumbs from both cake layers. Place one layer, top side down, on a flat serving plate. With an icing spatula, spread about a third of the frosting evenly on top. Place the other layer, top side down, on the first layer and press gently. Spread a thin layer of frosting over the entire cake to seal in any crumbs, then coat the cake with the remaining frosting. Serve immediately or keep covered at room temperature until ready to serve.

MAKES ONE 9-INCH (23-CM) CAKE, OR 10–12 SERVINGS

2¾ cups (12⅓ oz/385 g) all-purpose (plain) flour, plus extra for dusting

1 tablespoon baking powder

¼ teaspoon salt

¾ cup (6 oz/185 g) unsalted butter, at room temperature, plus extra for greasing

1¾ cups (12¼ oz/380 g) granulated sugar

3 large eggs, at room temperature

2 teaspoons vanilla extract (essence)

1¼ cups (10 fl oz/310 ml) buttermilk

FOR THE FROSTING:

4 oz (125 g) bittersweet chocolate, finely chopped

2 oz (60 g) unsweetened chocolate, finely chopped

1 cup (8 oz/250 g) unsalted butter, at room temperature

2 cups (8 oz/250 g) confectioners' (icing) sugar, sifted

3 tablespoons light corn syrup

1 teaspoon vanilla extract (essence)

Pinch of salt

TIRAMISÙ

MASCARPONE CHEESE

A very soft, smooth fresh Italian cheese made from cream, mascarpone is an essential ingredient in tiramisù. It has a consistency reminiscent of sour cream and is thick enough to spread when chilled, but sufficiently fluid to pour when at room temperature. Mascarpone is noted for its rich flavor and acidic tang and can be found sold in tubs in well-stocked food stores and in the cheese cases of Italian delicatessens.

Preheat the oven to 350°F (180°C). Lightly grease the bottom of a 9-inch (23-cm) round cake pan and line it with parchment (baking) paper. Lightly grease the paper and sides of the pan and then dust with flour.

To make the cake, in a bowl, whisk together the flour, baking powder, and salt until blended. In a large bowl, using a mixer on medium-high speed, beat the eggs until pale and thick, about 3 minutes. Add the sugar and vanilla and continue beating until very thick and tripled in volume, about 3 minutes more. Sprinkle the dry ingredients over the wet ingredients and, using a rubber spatula, fold gently until blended.

Pour into the prepared pan and spread evenly. Bake the cake until it springs back when lightly touched, about 30 minutes. Let cool on a rack for 15 minutes. Run a small knife around the inside of the pan to loosen the cake. Invert onto a cooling rack and lift off the pan. Carefully peel off the parchment paper. Let the cake cool completely.

To make the syrup, combine the water and the sugar in a small saucepan and cook over medium heat, stirring frequently, until the sugar dissolves. Bring to a boil and remove from the heat. Stir in the coffee liqueur and espresso powder. Set aside and cool to room temperature.

(Continued on next page.)

Unsalted butter for greasing

All-purpose (plain) flour for dusting

FOR THE CAKE:

1 cup (4½ oz/140 g) all-purpose (plain) flour

¾ teaspoon baking powder

¼ teaspoon salt

4 large eggs, at room temperature

⅔ cup (4⅔ oz/145 g) sugar

1¼ teaspoons vanilla extract (essence)

FOR THE SYRUP:

½ cup (4 fl oz/125 ml) water

⅓ cup (2⅓ oz/70 g) sugar

2 tablespoons coffee liqueur or dark rum

2 teaspoons instant espresso powder or instant coffee

FOR THE FILLING:

6 large egg yolks

⅓ cup (2⅓ oz/70 g) sugar

¼ cup (2 fl oz/60 ml) coffee liqueur or dark rum

1 tablespoon instant espresso powder or instant coffee powder

½ cup (4 fl oz/125 ml) heavy (double) cream

1½ cups (12 oz/375 g) mascarpone cheese

1½ teaspoons vanilla extract

Chocolate curls for garnish (page 105)

Unsweetened cocoa powder for garnish

To make the filling, in the top of a double boiler (page 106), whisk together the egg yolks, sugar, coffee liqueur, and espresso powder. Set over barely simmering water and beat with the mixer set on medium speed until very thick, about 6 minutes. Remove the top of the double boiler from the heat and set aside to cool, stirring frequently.

Meanwhile, in a bowl, using the mixer on medium-high speed, beat the cream until stiff peaks form when the beaters are lifted.

When the yolk mixture is cooled to room temperature, add the mascarpone and vanilla. Beat until smooth and well blended. Using the rubber spatula, fold in the whipped cream.

To assemble, cut the cake horizontally into 3 equal layers *(right)*. Remove the bottom of a 9-inch (23-cm) springform pan, close the ring, and set the ring on a flat serving plate. Place 1 cake layer in the springform ring. Generously brush and sprinkle with some of the syrup. Scoop about 1¾ cups (14 fl oz/430 ml) of the filling onto the layer and spread evenly. Place another cake layer on top of the filling, pressing gently. Generously brush and sprinkle with more of the syrup. Spread about 1¾ cups of the filling evenly over this layer. Place the third cake layer on top, pressing gently, then generously brush with syrup. Spread the remaining filling to cover the top. Holding the pan ring and plate together, gently tap against the counter to settle the ingredients. Cover with plastic wrap and refrigerate for at least 6 hours or up to overnight.

To serve, run a thin knife around the inside of the ring to loosen the cake. Unclasp and remove the ring. Garnish with chocolate curls, then sift a dusting of cocoa over the top. Slice and serve.

MAKES ONE 9-INCH (23-CM) CAKE. OR 12–16 SERVINGS

(Photograph appears on following page.)

SLICING CAKE LAYERS

To slice a single cake layer into thinner layers, set it on a work surface. Stand a ruler against the side of the cake and insert toothpicks horizontally into the cake side to divide the side into 3 equal sections. Repeat this process on the 3 other quadrants of the cake. Place one hand on top of the cake to hold it steady. Remove the top toothpick from one side and, using a long serrated knife and a slow sawing action, cut the cake parallel with the work surface, removing the toothpicks as you reach them with the knife. Remove the top layer and repeat.

CREPES SUZETTE

To make the crepes, combine the milk, flour, eggs, melted butter, granulated sugar, and salt in a blender. Blend until very smooth, about 1 minute. Pour the batter through a sieve set over a bowl. Cover and refrigerate the batter for 30 minutes or up to 1 day.

Set an 8-inch (20-cm) crepe pan over medium-low heat. Lightly grease the pan and pour in 2 tablespoons of the batter. Quickly swirl the pan to cover the bottom with the batter. Cook until the crepe is golden on the bottom side, about 1 minute. Carefully flip the crepe with a spatula. Cook until just beginning to brown in spots on the second side, another 30 seconds. Transfer to a plate and cover with a piece of waxed paper. Repeat with the remaining batter, greasing the pan when necessary and placing a layer of paper over each crepe. You should have 16 crepes in all. Use immediately, or cover and refrigerate for up to 1 day.

To make the filling, mix together the butter, confectioners' sugar, liqueur, and zest in a bowl until smooth. Place 1 crepe, speckled side up, on a work surface. Spread 1½ teaspoons filling on the top half of the crepe. Fold the bottom half over the filling, then fold again to form a triangle. Repeat with the remaining crepes and filling. Use immediately, or cover and refrigerate for up to 6 hours.

To make the sauce, pour the orange juice into a single large frying pan and set over medium-high heat. Bring to a boil and cook until reduced by about ½ cup (4 fl oz/125 ml). Reduce the heat to medium-low and slide all the folded crepes into the pan. Baste with the orange juice, then simmer gently until the crepes are warm, about 1 minute. Arrange the crepes on a serving platter and sprinkle the sugar over them. Pour the Grand Marnier and Cognac into a small saucepan and heat gently over low heat. Remove from the stove and carefully light with a long match. Pour the flaming liquid over the crepes and serve immediately, garnished with zest strips.

MAKES 16 FILLED CREPES, OR 8 SERVINGS

FLAMBÉING
Serving a flambéed dessert, such as crepes suzette, makes for a dramatic presentation. When liquor is ignited, some or most of the alcohol burns off, leaving behind a subtle flavor. Use a very small saucepan over low heat to warm the liquor until it is hot; do not allow it to boil. When you're ready to flambé, move the liquor away from the stove, and hold a lighted long kitchen match just over the warmed liquor to light the fumes rising from it. Keep long hair and loose sleeves out of the way, and keep a pan lid handy in case the flames flare up.

FOR THE CREPES:

1¼ cups (10 fl oz/310 ml) whole milk

1 cup (4½ oz/140 g) all-purpose (plain) flour

3 large eggs, at room temperature

2 tablespoons unsalted butter, melted, plus extra for greasing

1 tablespoon granulated sugar

¼ teaspoon salt

FOR THE FILLING:

½ cup (4 oz/125 g) unsalted butter, at room temperature

⅓ cup (1⅓ oz/40 g) confectioners' (icing) sugar

1 tablespoon Grand Marnier or other orange liqueur

1½ teaspoons finely grated orange zest, plus zest strips for garnish

FOR THE SAUCE:

1¾ cups (14 fl oz/430 ml) fresh orange juice

2 tablespoons granulated sugar

⅓ cup (3 fl oz/80 ml) Grand Marnier

2 tablespoons Cognac

FROZEN CITRUS MOUSSE

6 large eggs, separated, at room temperature

1½ cups (10½ oz/330 g) sugar, plus extra for dusting

¾ cup (6 fl oz/180 ml) fresh lemon juice

¼ teaspoon salt

1 teaspoon finely grated lemon zest

1 teaspoon finely grated lime zest

1 teaspoon finely grated orange zest

Unsalted butter for greasing

¾ cup (6 fl oz/180 ml) heavy (double) cream

In the top of a double boiler (page 106), whisk together the egg yolks, 1 cup (7 oz/220 g) of the sugar, the lemon juice, and the salt. Set over barely simmering water and cook, whisking constantly, until the mixture is thick enough to coat the back of a spoon, about 15 minutes. Remove the pan from the heat and stir in the zests. Scrape down the sides of the double boiler top and gently press a piece of plastic wrap directly onto the surface. Refrigerate or chill over an ice bath (page 66), stirring frequently, until thick.

While the lemon mixture is chilling, make room in the freezer for six ¾-cup (6–fl oz/180-ml) ramekins. Shape collars for the ramekins out of parchment (baking) paper or aluminum foil and tape to the ramekins *(right)*. Lightly grease the ramekins and collars. Dust with sugar. Place on a small baking sheet and set aside.

When the lemon mixture is well chilled, in a deep bowl, using a mixer on medium-high speed, whip the cream until firm peaks form when the beaters are lifted. Clean the beaters and, in another deep, clean bowl, beat the egg whites on medium-high speed until foamy. Gradually add the remaining ½ cup (3½ oz/105 g) sugar and continue to beat until firm peaks form when the beaters are lifted.

Whisk the chilled lemon mixture until smooth. Using a rubber spatula, scoop the whipped cream onto the lemon mixture and fold in until just blended. Add the whites and fold in gently until blended. Scoop into the prepared ramekins, gently tapping each ramekin against the counter to settle the contents.

Put the ramekins in the freezer for 30 minutes to set the mousse. Carefully cover with plastic wrap and freeze for at least 6 hours or up to overnight. Before serving, peel off the collars. Serve at once.

Note: This dish includes uncooked egg whites. For more information, see page 114.

MAKES 6 SERVINGS

COLLARS

Fitting a baking dish with a collar allows a mixture to rise above the rim of the dish. To make a collar, measure the circumference of the mold and cut a strip of parchment (baking) paper or aluminum foil 1–2 inches (2.5–5 cm) longer than the measure and 6–8 inches (15–20 cm) wide. Fold the strip in half lengthwise, wrap it around the dish—making sure that it extends 2½ inches (6 cm) above the rim—and secure it in place with tape.

WHITE CHOCOLATE AND RASPBERRY PARFAITS

In a bowl, using a mixer on medium speed, briefly beat together the mascarpone and heavy cream until smooth, about 10 seconds. Put the white chocolate in the top of a double boiler (page 106). Set over barely simmering water and melt, stirring until smooth. Add the still-hot melted white chocolate to the cream. Beat with the mixer on medium speed until well blended and slightly thickened, about 45 seconds. (If the white chocolate forms small lumps, briefly place the pan over simmering water again, then beat until smooth.)

Have ready six 9–fl oz (280-ml) long-stemmed wineglasses. Put 2 heaping tablespoons of the raspberries into the bottom of each glass. Spoon about 2 heaping tablespoons of the cream mixture over the berries. Sprinkle with 1 heaping tablespoon of the crushed cookies. Repeat with layers of the remaining fruit, cream mixture, and cookies, ending with cream. There should be 3 layers of fruit, 3 layers of cream, and 2 layers of crushed cookies.

Refrigerate for at least 2 hours or up to 8 hours (the longer the parfait chills, the more the cookie crumbs will soften). Garnish with a few raspberries, some crushed cookies, and the mint sprigs and serve at once.

MAKES 6 SERVINGS

1½ cups (12 oz/375 g) mascarpone cheese (page 78)

1 cup (8 fl oz/250 ml) heavy (double) cream

4 oz (125 g) white chocolate, coarsely chopped

3 cups (12 oz/375 g) raspberries, plus extra for garnish

18 amaretti di Saronno cookies *(far left),* coarsely crushed, plus extra crushed cookies for garnish

Fresh mint sprigs for garnish

AMARETTI

Amaretti di Saronno are delicate Italian cookies with a bitter almond flavor. They are packed in pairs and wrapped in colorful paper-thin tissue. These little cookies are very crunchy, light, and airy. To crush amaretti, place them in a heavy-duty plastic zippered bag and gently crush with the bottom of a cup or with a rolling pin. Be careful not to overdo it, as they can quickly turn to dust. A couple of passes and the crushed cookies will have the perfect coarse texture.

PANNA COTTA WITH STRAWBERRIES

Unsalted butter for greasing

1½ cups (12 fl oz/375 ml) whole milk

4 teaspoons unflavored powdered gelatin

½ cup (3½ oz/105 g) sugar

1½ cups (12 fl oz/375 ml) heavy (double) cream

1 teaspoon vanilla extract (essence)

Raspberry Coulis (page 113) for serving (optional)

6 large strawberries, stemmed and thinly sliced lengthwise

Lightly grease six ¾-cup (6–fl oz/180-ml) ramekins or custard cups and set on a small baking sheet.

Pour one-third of the milk into a saucepan and sprinkle in the gelatin. Let sit until the gelatin softens and swells, about 3 minutes. Add the remaining milk and the sugar and set the saucepan over medium heat. Cook, stirring constantly, until the sugar and gelatin are dissolved. Do not let the liquid boil. Remove from the heat and gently stir in the cream and vanilla until blended.

Divide the mixture evenly among the prepared ramekins. Cover with plastic wrap and refrigerate until well chilled and firm, at least 6 hours or up to overnight.

Up to 2 hours before serving, remove the ramekins from the refrigerator. Run a small kitchen towel under very hot water. Ring out the excess water. Fold the hot towel in half and lay it on the countertop. Place the ramekins on the towel to help release the bottoms. Carefully run a thin knife around the inside of each ramekin to loosen the custard. Invert and unmold each custard onto a small, flat serving plate. Drizzle with the coulis, if desired, and scatter the sliced strawberries over the top. Refrigerate until ready to serve.

MAKES 6 SERVINGS

USING GELATIN

Gelatin, an odorless, colorless, tasteless thickener derived from animal protein, is used to help many mousses, puddings, and other molded desserts hold their shape. It is used more rarely now than in past years, so many cooks are unfamiliar with its preparation. First, soften the gelatin in a small amount of cold liquid to help it dissolve evenly when combined with the rest of the ingredients in a recipe. Once softened, combine it with more liquid and warm it to activate its thickening power. (Do not let gelatin boil, or it will not set.) Finally, cool the mixture to let the gelatin take effect.

TRIFLE

In a bowl, whisk together the egg yolks, the ⅓ cup sugar, and the cornstarch until pale and well blended. Pour the cream into a small saucepan over medium heat and bring just to a boil. Gradually add the hot cream to the egg mixture while whisking. Return the mixture to the saucepan and cook over medium-low heat, whisking constantly, until just boiling and very thick, about 4 minutes. Pour it into a clean bowl and stir in the vanilla. Scrape down the sides and gently press a piece of plastic wrap directly onto the surface to prevent a skin from forming. Refrigerate until well chilled, at least 2 hours or up to overnight.

In a large bowl, toss together the berries, the rum, the zest, and the remaining 2 tablespoons sugar until well mixed. Cut each pound cake slice into 8 pieces. Arrange half of the cake pieces snugly in the bottom of a 2½-qt (2½-l) serving bowl. Spoon half of the berries along with half of the juices over the pound cake. Pour half of the chilled custard over the fruit. Top with layers of the remaining pound cake and the berries and their juices. Pour the remaining custard over the fruit. Cover with plastic wrap and refrigerate for at least 4 hours or up to 1 day.

Just before serving, top with whipped cream and garnish with the toasted almonds.

MAKES 10 SERVINGS

HANDLING BERRIES

Fresh raspberries, blackberries, blueberries, and strawberries need gentle handling. Since they are prone to mold, buy them close to the time you plan to serve them, and do not wash them in advance. When you're ready to use them, rinse them and lay them on a paper towel–lined baking sheet. Let them air-dry, or dry them by patting them very gently with another paper towel. If you have leftover berries you can't use right away, freeze them in a single layer on a baking sheet. When they are hard, put them in a plastic freezer bag or other container and freeze for up to 6 months.

4 large egg yolks, at room temperature

⅓ cup (2⅓ oz/70 g) plus 2 tablespoons sugar

2 teaspoons cornstarch (cornflour)

2 cups (16 fl oz/500 ml) heavy (double) cream

1 teaspoon vanilla extract (essence)

6 cups (1½ lb/750 g) mixed berries such as raspberries, blackberries, blueberries, and halved strawberries

3 tablespoons dark rum or sweet sherry

1 teaspoon finely grated lemon zest

6 slices Pound Cake (page 33), each ½ inch (12 mm) thick

Sweetened Whipped Cream (page 113) for serving

⅓ cup (1½ oz/75 g) sliced (flaked) almonds, toasted (page 115)

CHOCOLATE DECADENCE

The devotees of chocolate understand that it is no ordinary confection. A single bite of good chocolate can be comforting, cheering, even inspirational. The desserts in this chapter range from simple to sophisticated, but all are wonderfully chocolaty and richly indulgent. Don't try to choose from among the cookies and puddings, cakes and candies. Go ahead and try them all.

CHOCOLATE MOUSSE

In the top of a double boiler (page 106), combine the chocolate, butter, liqueur, water, and espresso powder, if using. Set over barely simmering water and melt the chocolate and butter, then whisk until the mixture is glossy and smooth. Remove from the heat and add the egg yolks one at a time, whisking well after each addition until blended. Add the vanilla, then continue stirring until the mixture is once again glossy and smooth. Set aside to cool, stirring frequently with a rubber spatula, until lukewarm, about 10 minutes.

In a bowl, using a mixer on medium speed, whip the cream until medium-firm peaks form when the beaters are lifted. Set aside. Carefully clean the beaters and, in another clean, bowl, combine the egg whites and salt. Beat the egg whites on medium-high speed until soft peaks form. Gradually add the sugar and continue to beat until glossy, firm peaks form.

Spoon the whipped cream onto the chocolate mixture and, using the rubber spatula, fold it in gently, stopping when large streaks of chocolate are still visible. Add the beaten egg whites and continue folding until the mousse is just blended.

Spoon into individual serving bowls or a single large bowl. Cover with plastic wrap and refrigerate for at least 4 hours or up to overnight before serving. Serve chilled with a dollop of whipped cream, white chocolate curls, and/or raspberries, if desired.

Note: This dish includes uncooked egg whites. For more information, see page 114.

MAKES 6–8 SERVINGS

FOLDING

The process of blending two mixtures (or ingredients) of different densities without losing volume or loft is known as folding. Scoop the lighter mixture on top of the heavier one and, using a rubber spatula, cut down through both of the mixtures to the bottom of the bowl. Using a circular motion, bring the spatula up along the side of the bowl farthest from you, lifting up some of the mixture from the bottom of the bowl and "folding" it over the top one. Rotate the bowl slightly and repeat. Continue until just blended, usually 6 or 7 times. Be careful not to overmix and deflate.

8 oz (250 g) bittersweet chocolate, finely chopped

¼ cup (2 oz/60 g) unsalted butter, cut into 3 equal pieces

3 tablespoons liqueur or spirits such as Kahlúa, brandy, or dark rum

2 tablespoons water

1 teaspoon instant espresso powder (optional)

4 large eggs, separated, at room temperature

1 teaspoon vanilla extract (essence)

¾ cup (6 fl oz/180 ml) heavy (double) cream

Pinch of salt

¼ cup (1¾ oz/50 g) sugar

Sweetened Whipped Cream (page 113), white chocolate curls (page 105), and/or raspberries for garnish (optional)

CHOCOLATE POTS DE CRÈME

1⅓ cups (11 fl oz/340 ml) heavy (double) cream

1⅓ cups (11 fl oz/340 ml) whole milk

6 oz (185 g) bittersweet chocolate, finely chopped

1 tablespoon instant espresso powder or instant coffee powder

6 large egg yolks

¼ cup (1¾ oz/50 g) sugar

Preheat the oven to 300°F (150°C). Have ready six ¾-cup (6–fl oz/ 180-ml) ramekins and a shallow roasting pan.

In a saucepan over medium-low heat, combine the cream, milk, chopped chocolate, and espresso powder and cook, whisking frequently, until the chocolate is melted and the liquid is hot. Do not allow to boil. Remove from the heat.

In a bowl, whisk together the egg yolks and sugar until well blended. While whisking constantly, gradually pour the hot chocolate mixture into the yolk mixture. Pour the custard through a sieve placed over a 4-cup (32–fl oz/1-l) glass measuring pitcher. Using a large spoon, skim off any foam and bubbles from the top.

Divide the custard evenly among the ramekins. Place the ramekins in the roasting pan and pour very hot tap water into the pan to come halfway up the sides of the cups. Cover the pan with aluminum foil.

Bake the custards until they are set but the centers still jiggle slightly when a cup is gently shaken, 55–60 minutes. Remove the pan from the oven and leave the ramekins in the water until cool enough to handle. Cover and refrigerate until well chilled, at least 2 hours or up to overnight. Serve chilled.

MAKES 6 SERVINGS

USING A WATER BATH
Delicate foods like custards, puddings, and mousses are protected from harsh oven heat by a water bath, also known as a *bain-marie*. Specialty water-bath pans are available, but it is easy to fashion one from your cupboard. All you need is a large, shallow pan to hold the dish or dishes containing the food. Once the dish(es) are in the pan, add hot water to the pan to reach halfway up their sides or as specified in a recipe. Sometimes the recipe will call for covering the pan. The food will cook gently and uniformly in a water bath without overheating.

PISTACHIO TRUFFLES

In the top of a double boiler (page 106), combine the chopped chocolate and cream. Set over barely simmering water and melt the chocolate, then whisk until the mixture is glossy and smooth. Remove from the heat and let cool to lukewarm, about 5 minutes, stirring occasionally. Add the butter pieces, stirring until smooth and well blended. Add the sour cream, vanilla, and salt and stir until blended. Let cool, stirring occasionally, until the chocolate just holds its shape when dropped from a spoon, about 40 minutes.

Line a small baking sheet with aluminum foil or parchment (baking) paper. Fit a pastry bag with a ½-inch (12-mm) plain tip. Fill the pastry bag with the chocolate mixture *(left)* and pipe into 1-inch (2.5-cm) mounds on the prepared baking sheet. Tap down any pointy tips with a dampened fingertip. Freeze the truffles until very firm, about 1½ hours.

Put the chopped pistachios in a small bowl. Remove a few truffles from the freezer. Roll each truffle in the nuts, pressing to coat. Don't worry about their irregular shapes: these truffles do not need to be perfectly round. The truffles should be served slightly chilled. Cover and refrigerate until ready to serve.

If desired, sift a light dusting of confectioners' sugar over the truffles just before serving.

MAKES 2 DOZEN 1-INCH (2.5-CM) TRUFFLES

4 oz (125 g) bittersweet chocolate, finely chopped

⅓ cup (3 fl oz/80 ml) heavy (double) cream

2 tablespoons unsalted butter, at room temperature, cut into 4 equal pieces

1 tablespoon sour cream

¼ teaspoon vanilla extract (essence)

Pinch of salt

1 cup (4 oz/125 g) medium-fine chopped unsalted pistachios

Confectioners' (icing) sugar for garnish (optional)

DOUBLE CHOCOLATE CHIP COOKIES

1 oz (30 g) unsweetened chocolate, coarsely chopped

1 cup (4½ oz/140 g) all-purpose (plain) flour

1½ teaspoons baking powder

¼ teaspoon salt

6 tablespoons (3 oz/90 g) unsalted butter, at room temperature

2 tablespoons vegetable shortening

⅔ cup (5⅓ oz/165 g) firmly packed light brown sugar

¼ cup (2 oz/60 g) granulated sugar

1 large egg, at room temperature

1 teaspoon vanilla extract (essence)

1 cup (6 oz/185 g) bitter-sweet or semisweet (plain) chocolate chips

½ cup (2 oz/60 g) coarsely chopped pecans or walnuts (optional)

Preheat the oven to 350°F (180°C) and line 2 baking sheets with parchment (baking) paper.

Put the chopped chocolate in the top of a double boiler (page 106). Set over simmering water and melt, whisking until smooth. Set aside to cool.

In a bowl, whisk together the flour, baking powder, and salt until blended. In another bowl, using a wooden spoon, beat together the butter, shortening, brown sugar, and granulated sugar until well blended and fluffy. Beat in the melted chocolate. Add the egg and vanilla and mix until blended. Add the dry ingredients and stir until almost blended. Add the chips and, if using, the nuts and continue stirring until blended.

Drop the dough by heaping tablespoonfuls onto the prepared baking sheets, spacing them about 1½ inches (4 cm) apart. Bake the cookies, 1 sheet at a time, until they are puffed but still look moist on top, about 15 minutes. Let the cookies cool on racks to room temperature. Serve immediately, or store in an airtight container at room temperature for up to 3 days.

MAKES 2 DOZEN COOKIES

VEGETABLE SHORTENING

These cookies, like many baked goods, call for using both butter and vegetable shortening. When cookie dough is made with butter alone, the cookies start to spread on the pan in the hot oven fairly quickly, because butter melts at a lower temperature than shortening. Cookies made with a combination of butter and shortening spread more slowly, resulting in a cookie with a thicker, puffier profile.

DEVIL'S FOOD CAKE WITH FUDGE FROSTING

FROSTING SAVVY

If the crust of a cake layer seems tough, or if the layer has an uneven top, trim it away with a serrated knife before frosting. To prevent the cut surface from shedding crumbs and spoiling the frosting, spread it with a thin layer of frosting (called the crumb layer) before applying the final frosting. To keep a serving plate clean while frosting a cake, place strips of waxed paper 4 inches (10 cm) wide in a square to cover the edges of the plate. Center the cake on the plate, making sure the strips are positioned to cover the plate all sides. Frost the cake and then carefully pull away the strips.

Preheat the oven to 350°F (180°C). Lightly grease the bottoms of two 9-by-2-inch (23-by-5-cm) round cake pans and line with parchment (baking) paper. Grease the paper and the sides of the pan and dust with flour. In a large bowl, sift together the flour, cocoa, baking powder, baking soda, and salt. In another large bowl, using a mixer on medium speed, beat the butter until smooth. Gradually add the brown sugar and continue beating until fluffy. Beat in the vanilla. Add the eggs one at a time, beating well after each addition. Add the flour mixture in 3 batches alternately with the buttermilk in 2 batches, mixing on low speed after each addition.

Divide the batter between the prepared pans and spread it out evenly. Tap the pans gently on the counter to dispel air pockets. Bake until a toothpick inserted in the center of a cake comes out clean, 25–30 minutes. Let cool on a rack for 15 minutes. Run a small knife around the inside of the pans to loosen the layers. Invert onto the rack and lift off the pans, then carefully peel off the parchment paper. Let the layers cool completely before frosting.

To make the frosting, in the top part of a double boiler (page 106), combine the chocolate and heavy cream. Set over barely simmering water until the chocolate melts, then whisk until well blended. Let cool slightly. Add the sour cream and salt and stir just until blended. Set aside, stirring occasionally, until room temperature. Whisk the frosting briefly until lighter in color and thick enough to spread.

To assemble, brush away any loose crumbs from both layers. Place one cake layer, top side down, on a flat serving plate. With an icing spatula, spread about a third of the frosting on top. Place the other cake layer, top side down, on the first layer and press gently. Spread a thin layer of frosting over the entire cake to seal in any crumbs, then thickly coat the cake with the remaining frosting. Serve at once or keep covered at room temperature until ready to serve.

MAKES ONE 9-INCH (23-CM) CAKE, OR 10–12 SERVINGS

2⅓ cups (10½ oz/330 g) all-purpose (plain) flour, plus extra for dusting

1 cup (3 oz/90 g) unsweetened cocoa powder, sifted

1½ teaspoons baking powder

½ teaspoon baking soda (bicarbonate of soda)

½ teaspoon salt

¾ cup (6 oz/185 g) unsalted butter, at room temperature, plus extra for greasing

2 cups (1 lb/500 g) firmly packed light brown sugar

2 teaspoons vanilla extract (essence)

4 large eggs, at room temperature

1½ cups (12 fl oz/375 ml) buttermilk, at room temperature

FOR THE FROSTING:

12 oz (375 g) bittersweet chocolate, finely chopped

1¾ cups (14 fl oz/430 ml) heavy (double) cream

½ cup (4 oz/125 g) sour cream

Pinch of salt

CHOCOLATE CHEESECAKE

FOR THE CRUST:

1½ cups (4½ oz/140 g) chocolate cookie crumbs (from about 30 crisp chocolate wafers)

3 tablespoons sugar

¼ cup (2 oz/60 g) unsalted butter, melted

FOR THE FILLING:

8 oz (250 g) bittersweet chocolate, finely chopped

3 packages (8 oz/250 g each) cream cheese, at room temperature

3 tablespoons all-purpose (plain) flour

¼ teaspoon salt

¾ cup (5¼ oz/160 g) sugar

¼ cup (2 oz/60 g) sour cream, at room temperature

1½ teaspoons vanilla extract (essence)

3 large eggs, at room temperature

Chocolate curls, for garnish (far right)

To make the crust, preheat the oven to 400°F (200°C). Lightly grease a 9-inch (23-cm) springform pan. In a bowl, combine the cookie crumbs, sugar, and melted butter. Stir until the mixture is well blended and the crumbs are evenly moist. Pour into the springform pan and press evenly onto the bottom and about 1½ inches (4 cm) up the sides of the pan (page 18). Bake until set, about 10 minutes. Let cool on a rack. Reduce the oven temperature to 300°F (150°C).

To make the filling, put the chocolate in the top of a double boiler (page 106). Set over barely simmering water until the chocolate melts, then remove from the heat and stir until smooth. Set aside to cool.

In a large bowl, combine the cream cheese, flour, and salt. Using a mixer on medium to medium-high speed, beat until very smooth and fluffy, stopping and scraping down the sides frequently. Add the cooled chocolate, sugar, sour cream, and vanilla. Beat until well blended, again scraping down the sides frequently. Add the eggs one at a time, beating well after each addition, until just blended. Pour into the crust and spread out evenly.

Bake until the filling is set but the center still jiggles slightly when gently shaken (it will firm as it cools), 60–70 minutes. The edges will be slightly puffed. Let cool on a rack to room temperature. Cover and refrigerate until well chilled (overnight is best).

To serve, unclasp and remove the pan sides, then run a long, thin knife between the pan bottom and the crust. Carefully slide the cake onto a flat serving plate. Using a thin-bladed knife, cut into slices, dipping the knife in hot water and wiping it dry before the next cut. Garnish each slice with chocolate curls and serve.

MAKES ONE 9-INCH (23-CM) CHEESECAKE, OR 16 SERVINGS

CHOCOLATE CURLS
To make decorative chocolate curls, use a vegetable peeler to shave the edge (for narrow curls) or side (for wide curls) of a bar of chocolate. The bigger the chunk of chocolate, the wider the curls will be. To ensure long, handsome curls rather than stubby shavings, the chocolate must be room temperature or even slightly warm. Try first rubbing the chocolate with your palm or, for larger chunks, microwave on low for about 5 seconds and repeat as necessary. Refrigerate the curls until ready to use, or keep at room temperature for a short amount of time.

WARM MOLTEN CHOCOLATE CAKES

Preheat the oven to 400°F (200°C). Lightly grease six ¾-cup (6–fl oz/ 180-ml) ramekins and dust with cocoa. Set the ramekins on a small baking sheet.

In the top of a double boiler *(left)*, combine the chocolate and butter. Set over barely simmering water and melt, then whisk until the mixture is glossy and smooth. Remove from the heat and stir in the vanilla and salt, then set aside to cool slightly.

In a large bowl, using a mixer on medium-high speed, beat together the egg yolks, half of the sugar, the 2 tablespoons cocoa, and the zest, if using, until thick. Spoon the chocolate mixture into the yolk mixture and beat until well blended. The mixture will be very thick.

In a bowl, using clean beaters, beat the egg whites on medium-high speed until very foamy and thick. Sprinkle in the remaining sugar and increase the speed to high. Continue beating until firm, glossy peaks form. Spoon half of the beaten whites onto the chocolate mixture and whisk in until just blended. Add the remaining whites and stir gently until just blended. Spoon into the prepared ramekins, dividing evenly.

Bake the cakes until they are puffed and the tops are cracked, 13 minutes. The inside of the cracks will look very wet. Remove from the oven and serve immediately in the ramekins. Or, run a small knife around inside of each ramekin to loosen the cake and invert the cakes onto individual plates. Serve with a drizzle of raspberry coulis or crème anglaise, if desired.

Variation Tip: If you would like your molten chocolate cakes to have crunchy bottoms and sides, dust the greased ramekins with superfine (caster) sugar in place of the cocoa powder.

MAKES 6 SERVINGS

DOUBLE BOILERS

A double boiler cooks foods gently on the stove top. Consisting of two nesting saucepans, double boilers are widely available, but a makeshift one is easy to assemble *(above)*. Choose a saucepan and a heatproof bowl that rests securely in the top. Fill the saucepan with water to a depth of 1–2 inches (2.5–5 cm). Once the bowl is placed atop the pan, the water must not touch it. Remember that boiling water bubbles up, so check the water level before setting the bowl in place. Bring the water to a boil, set the bowl in place, and reduce the heat so that the water simmers gently.

8 oz (250 g) bittersweet chocolate, finely chopped

¼ cup (2 oz/60 g) unsalted butter, cut into pieces, plus extra for greasing

1 teaspoon vanilla extract (essence)

Pinch of salt

4 large egg yolks

6 tablespoons (2½ oz/75 g) sugar

2 tablespoons Dutch-process cocoa powder (page 114), sifted, plus extra for dusting

1 teaspoon finely grated orange zest (optional)

3 large egg whites, at room temperature

Raspberry Coulis (page 113) or Crème Anglaise (page 113) for serving (optional)

DESSERT BASICS

Any occasion can be made more special by ending it with a homemade dessert. The recipes in this cookbook can star in a birthday celebration, make a sweet ending to a dinner party, or brighten up a rainy afternoon. Whatever the reason, a cake, tart, or batch of cookies fresh from the oven is always irresistible. And the welcome reception that is sure to greet a sweet is enough to make any cook proud. Following are some basic tips on preparing different desserts.

GETTING STARTED

Before you begin making any recipe, and especially a baking recipe where precision is important, it is a good idea to read all the way through the directions before you begin. Make sure you understand all the steps and have every ingredient and piece of equipment on hand. Next, gather and prepare all your ingredients. (The French term for this advance preparation is *mise en place*, or "putting in place.") For dessert recipes, this may mean preheating the oven, greasing or lining a pan, and having all your wet and dry ingredients measured out in bowls or containers beforehand, just as a recipe specifies.

Some recipes will call for certain ingredients at different temperatures. For example, butter should be at room temperature if you are making cookies, but it should be very cold if you are making pastry dough. Also be aware that cold eggs fresh from the refrigerator are easier to separate, while those at room temperature are easier to whip up.

MEASURING

Accuracy is crucial when measuring ingredients for the exact chemistry of baking. Every baker should have both dry and wet measuring cups, which are not quite the same thing. Dry measuring cups are a nesting set of cups usually made of plastic or stainless steel. Once you have filled the cup with the dry ingredient, use the back of a knife blade to level it out flush with the top of the cup, giving an exact amount. Liquid measuring cups look like pitchers and are usually made of clear glass or plastic. When measuring a liquid, place the cup on a flat surface, let the liquid settle, then read it at eye level.

Certain ingredients require extra care when measuring. Brown sugar should be packed into a cup firmly enough that it retains the cup's shape when tapped out. Lightly rinsing a cup with cold water before pouring in a sticky ingredient such as honey or molasses will help it slip out easily. A recipe will sometimes call for sifting flour or confectioners' (icing) sugar before or after measuring, to aerate it.

OVEN SAVVY

An accurate heat level is also very important when baking. Use an oven thermometer to determine your oven's accuracy. If the oven is off by 25° or 50°F (5° or 10°C), adjust the temperature knob accordingly.

Most recipes are designed for baking on oven racks as close to the center of the oven as possible. If you are baking a dessert such as cookies or a layer cake that will not all fit on one rack, place the racks as close to the center of the oven as possible.

Do not open the oven door during baking until it's time to check for doneness. A considerable amount of heat escapes every time the oven door is opened. Also, banging an oven door shut can cause delicate desserts such as a cake or soufflé to fall. Do begin checking 8–10 minutes before the item is supposed to be done.

COOKIES

Two types of cookies are included in this book: drop cookies, such as Double Chocolate Chip Cookies (page 101), and bar cookies, such as Brownies (page 30) and Lemon Curd Squares (page 37).

CREAMING BUTTER

A recipe for cookie dough or cake batter typically starts with creaming the butter. This means that the butter should be beaten until it lightens in color, increases in volume, and is as smooth and fluffy as possible. Creaming aerates the butter and contributes to a light texture. This step will take 3–4 minutes with an electric mixer, or longer by hand with a wooden spoon.

FORMING COOKIES

To make drop cookies, scoop up a tablespoonful of batter and use a second spoon to push it off onto a baking sheet, spacing the cookies about 1½ inches (4 cm) apart on all sides. Do not crowd too many cookies on a sheet for each batch.

If baking more than one sheet of cookies at a time, it's a good idea to switch the baking sheets from the upper to lower rack and rotate them back to front halfway through the baking time to ensure even browning.

PIES AND TARTS

Whether filled with fresh berries or a rich custard, a light, flaky crust is one of the most important elements in a pie or tart. Pies are usually baked in a pie plate with sloping sides and may include both a bottom and top crust. Tarts are baked in a straight-sided tart pan and almost always have only a bottom crust. A recipe for Basic Pastry Dough appears on page 113 and can be used for the pie and tart recipes throughout this book.

CUTTING IN BUTTER

The flaky texture of pie and tart pastry comes from properly cutting butter and/or another fat into flour. The fat is reduced to the texture of small peas or coarse meal by repeated slicing with a pastry blender or two knives. The fat should be cold to start with and should be worked quickly to prevent it from warming up and softening. The small bits of cold fat in the rolled-out dough will melt once the pie is baked, releasing steam and creating airy layers within the crust.

ROLLING OUT THE CRUST

To prepare dough for rolling, use your hands to shape the dough into a flat, round disk and chill it to "relax" the dough and prevent shrinking. Place the disk on the work surface and tap it with the rolling pin to flatten and spread it out a bit. Before rolling out your crust, sprinkle flour lightly over both the work surface and the rolling pin. Add flour beneath the dough and on the rolling pin as you work, to help prevent sticking. Shown opposite are the basic steps for rolling out a crust:

1 Rolling the dough: Starting with the pin in the center of the disk, roll it away from you toward the far edge. Stop rolling and lift the pin at a finger's width from the edge of the dough. Bring the pin back to the center of the disk and roll it toward you, again stopping just shy of the edge. Give the dough a quarter turn and repeat. Use firm and steady pressure as you roll, and work quickly. Repeat turning and rolling until the dough is about ⅛ inch (3 mm) thick, with 1 inch (2.5 cm) to spare around the pan's circumference for pies or ½ inch (12 mm) for tarts.

2 Trimming a circle: Place your pie or tart pan in the center of the dough circle and, with a small knife, trim the dough into a neat circle, including the extra ½ inch (12 mm) or 1 inch (2.5 cm) around the outside of the pan.

3 Transferring the dough: Roll the round of dough loosely around the rolling pin and unroll it over the pie or tart pan, draping it loosely over the top of the pan.

4 Fitting the dough into the pan: Lift up the edges of the dough circle as you gently ease it into the contours of the pan, being careful not to stretch the dough.

CAKES

Many of the most special celebrations in life—from birthdays to weddings—call for cakes. The techniques that follow will help you prepare a cake with successful results.

MIXING BATTER

As with cookies, once the butter is creamed for a cake batter, sugar is added and beaten in until the sugar grains are fully incorporated (the mixture should no longer feel gritty if rubbed between your fingertips). Now the mixture becomes a batter, and other ingredients, such as flour and eggs, are stirred in. Add eggs one at a time, beating well after each addition.

Do not overmix a batter, or you may destroy the air bubbles that are created during the creaming stage. Mix it just until the flour is no longer visible. For more details on folding ingredients into a batter, see page 94.

GREASING AND DUSTING PANS

While some cakes, such as angel food cake, are baked in dry pans, most cake recipes call for greasing pans with butter and dusting them with flour or cocoa. It is generally a good idea to line the pan as well. This keeps the cake from sticking to the pan.

To grease a pan, rub the inside bottom and sides of the pan with butter. To line a pan, cut a parchment (baking) paper round or rectangle that will fit snugly in the bottom of the pan. Lay the paper form in the pan and grease it as well. Next, sprinkle some flour on the pan's sides and bottom (or its paper lining). Holding the pan over the sink or work surface, turn and tilt the pan to distribute the flour evenly. Gently tap the excess flour from the pan. If you are baking a chocolate cake that won't be frosted, use cocoa powder in place of flour to avoid a contrasting white dusting on the brown cake.

CUSTARDS

Custard is a mixture of eggs and milk or cream cooked just until the proteins in the ingredients thicken to form a soft, smooth, satiny dish. Examples of custard recipes in this book include Chocolate Pots de Crème (page 97) and Crème Brûlée (page 21). They are first cooked on the stove top and then in the oven and are often served in ramekins.

Custard sauces, or stirred custards, are made from milk or cream, eggs, and sugar. They are cooked only on the stove top, resulting in a pourable consistency. One of the best-known custard sauces is crème anglaise (see page 113). Many ice creams are simply frozen versions of crème anglaise.

TEMPERING EGGS

When making custard, you must handle the eggs carefully. If eggs are heated up very quickly and suddenly, they will curdle, resulting in a texture similar to that of scrambled eggs. For a silky custard texture, the eggs must be tempered, or heated gradually. A splash of hot liquid is stirred into the eggs before they are poured into a hot pan on the stove top. Constant stirring as the eggs heat also helps keep the process slow and gradual.

COOLING AND UNMOLDING

Baked goods are often set on racks so that air can circulate around them as they cool.

For cakes, set the pan on a wire rack and let cool for at least 10 minutes or as directed in a recipe. Loosen the sides of the cake with a thin knife, place a wire rack on top of the cake, and carefully invert the cake in its pan, using potholders if the pan is still hot. If the pan doesn't lift easily from the cake, give it a slight shake. The cake should fall from the pan. Peel the parchment paper from the bottom of the cake and discard. Let the cake cool completely before frosting. For more information on frosting a cake, see page 102.

BASIC RECIPES

Here are several basic elements used in the recipes in this book.

BASIC PASTRY DOUGH

1¼ cups (5¾ oz/175 g) all-purpose (plain) flour

1 tablespoon sugar

½ teaspoon salt

¼ cup (2 oz/60 g) cold unsalted butter, cut into ¾-inch (2-cm) pieces

3 tablespoons cold vegetable shortening, cut into ¾-inch (2-cm) pieces

3 tablespoons very cold water

To make the dough in a food processor, combine the flour, sugar, and salt in the bowl. Pulse to blend. Add the pieces of butter and shortening and pulse until reduced to ½-inch (12-mm) pieces. Add the water a little at a time and pulse until the dough just begins to come together in a rough mass.

To make the dough by hand, combine the flour, sugar, and salt in a bowl. Add the pieces of butter and shortening and toss to coat with flour. Using a pastry blender or 2 knives, cut the pieces of fat into the flour mixture until they are no larger than small peas. Dribble the water over the mixture and toss with a fork until the dough is evenly moist and begins to come together in a rough mass.

Remove the dough to a work surface and shape into a 5-inch (13-cm) disk. Wrap in plastic and refrigerate until well chilled, at least 2 hours. Makes enough dough for 1 single-crust pie, tart, or galette.

RASPBERRY COULIS

3 cups (12 oz/375 g) raspberries

¼ cup (1 oz/30 g) confectioners' (icing) sugar, plus more as needed

1 teaspoon fresh lemon juice

In a food processor, combine the raspberries and confectioners' sugar. Pulse until the berries are puréed. Pass the purée through a fine-mesh sieve placed over a small bowl, pressing on the contents of the sieve with the back of a wooden spoon to extract all the juice. Stir in the lemon juice. Taste and add more sugar, if desired. Makes about 1 cup (8 fl oz/250 ml).

SWEETENED WHIPPED CREAM

¾ cup (6 fl oz/180 ml) heavy (double) cream, well chilled

2 tablespoons sugar

½ teaspoon vanilla extract (essence)

In a deep bowl, combine the cream, sugar, and vanilla. Using an electric mixer set on medium-high speed, beat until soft peaks form and the cream is billowy, about 2 minutes. Cover the bowl and refrigerate until serving or for up to 2 hours. Makes 1½ cups (12 fl oz/375 ml).

CRÈME ANGLAISE

1¼ cups (10 fl oz/310 ml) milk

5 large egg yolks

¼ cup (2 oz/60 g) sugar

2 tablespoons Grand Marnier or other orange liqueur (optional)

1 teaspoon vanilla extract (essence)

In a saucepan over medium heat, heat the milk until small bubbles appear along the edge. Meanwhile, in a bowl, whisk together the egg yolks and sugar until pale and thick. Slowly add the hot milk while whisking. Return the mixture to the saucepan over medium heat. Cook, stirring constantly, until the mixture is thick enough to coat the back of a spoon, about 5 minutes. Pour through a sieve set over a clean bowl. Stir in the liqueur, if desired, and vanilla. Cover and refrigerate. Makes about 1½ cups (12 fl oz/375 ml).

GLOSSARY

BAKING POWDER VS. BAKING SODA
Baking powder and soda are chemical leaveners. They work by reacting with both liquids and heat to release carbon dioxide gas, which in turn leavens a batter, causing it to rise as it cooks. Baking powder is a mixture of an acid and an alkaline, or base, that is activated when it is exposed to moisture or heat. Double-acting baking powder contains two acids. The first reacts while mixing the batter, and the second reacts in the oven during the baking process.

Baking soda, also called bicarbonate of soda, is an alkaline, or base, that releases carbon dioxide gas only when it comes into contact with an acidic ingredient, such as sour cream, yogurt, buttermilk, or citrus juice.

BUTTER, UNSALTED Also called sweet butter, unsalted butter is favored for baking. It lacks the additional salt that can interfere with the taste of the final recipe and is likely to be fresher since salt acts as a preservative.

BUTTERMILK A form of cultured low-fat or nonfat milk, buttermilk adds a tangy flavor and thick, creamy texture to batters and doughs. Its acidity also gives a boost to leavening agents.

CAKE PAN Round pans, generally 2 inches (5 cm) deep and 8 or 9 inches (20 or 23 cm) in diameter, used especially for baking cakes. You will want to have at least two on hand for making layer cakes.

CHOCOLATE, MELTING To melt chocolate, chop it into chunks and place it in the top pan of a double boiler (page 106) set over barely simmering water. Make sure the water does not touch the bottom of the top pan and do not let the water boil. Any moisture or steam that comes in contact with the chocolate could cause it to seize, or stiffen. As it melts, stir the chocolate with a wooden spoon. When the chocolate is liquefied, remove the top of the double boiler from the bottom and set aside.

To melt chocolate in a microwave, place the chunks in a microwave-safe dish and heat on low. Check it after 1 minute and every 30 or 40 seconds thereafter to prevent scorching. When the chocolate is shiny and soft, remove it. Although it will not melt completely, it will become smooth and liquid upon stirring. For more information about chocolate varieties, see page 30.

COCOA POWDER This powder is made by removing nearly all the cocoa butter from chocolate liquor and then grinding it to an unsweetened powder. Alkalized, or Dutch-processed, cocoa powder is milder and more soluble than nonalkalized. Nonalkalized or natural cocoa powder is lighter in color but bolder in flavor than alkalized. Use the variety specified in the recipe; if none is specified, either will work.

CORN SYRUP This syrup, made from cornstarch, is a common commercial sweetener, but it can also be used in home cooking and baking. Available in dark and light versions, it adds moisture and chewiness to cakes and cookies.

CREAM OF TARTAR This white powder is potassium tartrate, a by-product of wine making. It is used to stabilize egg whites so that they whip up more easily. Cream of tartar also inhibits sugar from crystallizing, adds creaminess to frosting, and contributes to whiter, finer crumbs and greater loft in cakes. It is also mixed with baking soda to create baking powder.

EGG, RAW Eggs are sometimes used raw in mousses and other preparations. Raw eggs run a risk of being infected with salmonella or other bacteria, which can lead to food poisoning. This risk is of most concern to small children, older people, pregnant women, and anyone with a compromised immune system. If you have health and safety concerns, do not consume raw egg.

ESPRESSO POWDER, INSTANT This powder can add the full flavor of espresso roast coffee beans to many desserts. Look for it in the coffee section of well-stocked food stores or at specialty coffee stores or Italian delicatessens.

FLOUR

All-Purpose: Also known as plain flour, all-purpose flour is the popular general-use flour that is good for a wide range of desserts. It is made from a mixture of soft and hard wheats.

Cake: Low in protein and high in starch, cake flour is milled from soft wheat and contains cornstarch. It is very fine in texture and has also undergone a bleaching process that increases its ability to hold water and sugar. Cakes made with cake flour are less likely to fall.

NUTS, TOASTING To toast nuts, preheat the oven to 325°F (165°C). Spread the nuts in a single layer on a baking sheet. Place the sheet in the oven and toast, stirring occasionally, until the nuts are fragrant, lightly browned, and coated in a layer of their own oil. Depending on the type and size of the nuts, this may take 10–20 minutes. Remove the nuts from the pan as soon as they start to brown, pouring them onto a plate and letting cool. They will continue to cook slightly after removal from the pan. Or, toast nuts in a small, dry frying pan over medium heat. Shake the pan often, and remove the nuts when they start to brown.

PASTRY BLENDER This tool, used to cut butter and other fats into flour for flaky pastry crusts, consists of a sturdy handle anchoring a row of wires or blades. The wires cut the fat into smaller and smaller pieces until it resembles small peas.

PUDDING MOLD A mold with a tight-fitting lid used for making steamed puddings. Pudding molds are usually round with a tube in the center for even heating. Often, the sides and tops are decoratively fluted. The mold is set in a hot water bath while the pudding steams.

SPRINGFORM PAN A deep, round cake pan with sides secured by a clamp, this pan is useful for cheesecakes and other solid cakes. The sides release when the clamp is released, making the cake easy to remove. A 9-inch (23-cm) diameter is the size most commonly used. Generally, springform pans should be used atop baking sheets to prevent batter from leaking onto the bottom of the oven.

SUGAR

Brown: Rich in flavor, brown sugar is granulated sugar colored with molasses. It has a soft, moist texture and comes in mild-flavored light brown and strong-flavored dark brown varieties.

Confectioners': Also called powdered or icing sugar, confectioners' sugar is granulated sugar that has been crushed to a powder and mixed with a little cornstarch (cornflour).

Granulated: The most common sugar is granulated white sugar, which has been extracted from sugarcane or beets and refined by boiling, centrifuging, chemical treatment, and straining. For baking recipes, buy only sugar that is specifically labeled cane sugar; beet sugar may have an unpredictable effect.

Superfine: When finely ground, granulated sugar becomes superfine sugar, also known as caster sugar. Because it dissolves rapidly, it is preferred for delicate mixtures such as beaten egg whites. To make your own, process granulated sugar in a food processor until finer granules form.

WHIPPING A process by which air is incorporated into a food, whipping increases the volume of ingredients such as heavy (double) cream or egg whites. These ingredients are often used to lighten the texture of heavy mixtures. Whipping can be accomplished using a wire whisk, an electric mixer, or a rotary beater. For soft peaks, the whipped ingredient will gently fall to one side when the beater or whisk is lifted. Firm peaks will hold their shape and stand upright. See also page 67.

VANILLA EXTRACT Also known as vanilla essence, this distillation lends perfume, depth, and nuance to many recipes. Avoid imitation vanilla, which is made of artificial flavorings and has an inferior taste. The best vanilla extracts identify the type of bean used. There are three common types of vanilla beans: Tahitian, Mexican, and Bourbon-Madagascar. Mexican and Bourbon-Madagascar beans are more strongly scented, while Tahitian are more delicate. For information on selecting and preparing whole vanilla beans, see page 21.

INDEX

SIMON & SCHUSTER SOURCE
A Division of Simon & Schuster Inc.
Rockefeller Center
1230 Avenue of the Americas
New York, NY 10020

WILLIAMS-SONOMA
Founder and Vice-Chairman: Chuck Williams
Book Buyer: Cecilia Michaelis

WELDON OWEN INC.
Chief Executive Officer: John Owen
President: Terry Newell
Chief Operating Officer: Larry Partington
Vice President, International Sales: Stuart Laurence
Creative Director: Gaye Allen
Series Editor: Sarah Putman Clegg
Associate Editor: Heather Belt
Production Manager: Chris Hemesath
Photograph Editor: Lisa Lee

Weldon Owen wishes to thank the following people
for their generous assistance and support in producing
this book: Copy Editor Sharon Silva; Consulting Editor
Norman Kolpas; Designer Douglas Chalk; Food Stylists
Kim Konecny and Erin Quon; Prop Stylist Carol Hacker;
Photographer's Assistant Faiza Ali; Assistant Photograph
Editor Kris Ellis; Proofreaders Desne Ahlers and
Carrie Bradley; Indexer Ken DellaPenta; and
Production Designer Joan Olson.

The author wishes to thank Katherine Seeley,
Linda Wesley, and, as always, the staff of *Fine Cooking*
magazine for their constant support and encouragement.

Williams-Sonoma Collection *Dessert* was
conceived and produced by Weldon Owen Inc.,
814 Montgomery Street, San Francisco,
California 94133, in collaboration with
Williams-Sonoma, 3250 Van Ness Avenue,
San Francisco, California 94109.

A Weldon Owen Production
Copyright © 2002 by Weldon Owen Inc. and
Williams-Sonoma Inc.

Set in Trajan, Utopia, and Vectora.

Color separations by Bright Arts Graphics
Singapore (Pte.) Ltd.
Printed and bound in Singapore by Tien Wah Press
(Pte.) Ltd.

First printed in 2002.

For information about special discounts for bulk
purchases, please contact Simon & Schuster
Special Sales: 1-800-456-6798 or
business@simonandschuster.com

10 9 8 7 6 5 4 3 2

Library of Congress Cataloging-in-Publication Data

Dodge, Abigail Johnson.
 Dessert / recipes and text, Abigail Johnson
Dodge ; general editor, Chuck Williams ;
photographs, Maren Caruso.
  p. cm. — (Williams-Sonoma collection)
  1. Desserts. I. Williams, Chuck. II. Title.
III. Williams-Sonoma collection (New York, N.Y.)

TX773 .D625 2002
641.8'6—dc21

2001042886

ISBN 0-7432-2643-7

A NOTE ON WEIGHTS AND MEASURES

All recipes include customary U.S. and metric measurements. Metric conversions are based on
a standard developed for these books and have been rounded off. Actual weights may vary.